Howard Butt is Vice-Chairman of the Board, H. E. Butt Grocery Company of Corpus Christi, Texas. An active lay preacher, Mr. Butt also directs inter-denominational ministries through the Laity Lodge Foundation and Christian Men, Incorporated. He has served on boards and commissions for various Christian educational institutions and evangelistic associations. Mr. Butt is married and the father of three children. THE VELVET COVERED BRICK is his first book.

Brooner Studio, Corpus Christi

THE VELVET COVERED BRICK

THE VELVET COVERED BRICK

Christian Leadership in an Age of Rebellion

Howard Butt

Harper & Row, Publishers

New York, Evanston, San Francisco, London

6478

Designed by Janice Stern

Library of Congress Cataloging in Publication Data

Butt, Howard E. Jr.
  The velvet covered brick.
  Includes bibliographical references.
  1. Christian leadership.   I.   Title.
BV652.1.B87   1973   248   72–11352
ISBN 0–06–061258–4

To my Father and my Brother,
whose leadership makes mine possible

Contents

Foreword

Revolutionists will say this book is counter-revolutionary. It is; in their saying so they will be correct. Don't misunderstand: I am a rebel myself, no doubt about that. If I were young or black or poor I might out-Afro Angela Davis, out-growl the Black Panthers, and out-revolt Herbert Marcuse writing about it. Since I'm middle-aged, affluent, and suntan-white, that's only speculation. My rebellion has been deeper, more subtle, more hidden, less honest than theirs. For all of us the issue is not whether revolution is understandable. Revolution—in human history—is understandable always. Revolution should never surprise us—it is nothing new. This is a book about Authority and Submission, the way to think that *is* new. My own personal story starts the book, is integral in its development, and is woven throughout. For you I am writing: "The Confessions of a Businessman."

In the summer of 1972, when Sargent Shriver accepted the Democratic vice-presidential nomination, he quoted Pierre Teilhard de Chardin: "Some day, after we have mastered the winds, the waves, the tides, and gravity, we will harness for God the energies of love: and then for the second time in the history of the world man will have discovered fire!" In tongues of fire at Pentecost the way has been lit. Love's terrible fire burns, cleanses, destroys, consumes us. Love's warm flame opens, melts, unites, fulfills us. Man's second discovery of fire is in the Christian doctrine of organization: Authority and Submission.

"Submission" is a loaded word—also "Authority." But clear thinking demands I use them. We live in an age of romanticized revolution. We are rebels, we humans, all of us; this fact about us is old. Now we face—as if it were new—revolution intellectual-ized, rebellion as a conceptual system. In religious language you could describe it as Revolution Idolized. Or, from Hollywood, Rebellion as Glamour. Our current crisis proceeds directly from these ideas, these concepts, this thinking. Oppression on the top is one and the same thing as revolution on the bottom. Repression on top produces rebellion below; rebellion below produces repres-sion on top. Hair gets longer; tempers get shorter. Wider and wider whirls the dynamite of social despair . . . faster and faster, deeper and deeper, hotter and hotter. The social crucible spins glowing red. I cannot forget Mrs. Parkinson's sly law: "Heat Pro-duced By Pressure Expands To Fill The Mind Available From Which It Can Only Pass To A Cooler Mind."[1] In a revolutionary age Authority and Submission offer us the thinking of God's cool mind.

"How to Change the Establishment" could be my alternate title. Underneath (on the bottom) the issue is whether revolution is right or wrong, wise or unwise, good or bad. On the top (in leadership) the issue is whether the Establishment can change and truly be different. If you are a revolutionary you cannot change the Establishment. If you are a leader you cannot change the revolu-tionaries. You can change no one but yourself. *On the top* and *underneath* get called to change together. When revolutionists change, the Establishment changes too, unnoticed. When leaders change, rebels relax too, just when you expect it least. What matters is not the Establishment; what matters is not the Revolu-tion; what matters is the everloving truth

This book is an unfolding of one rebel's story. It has been written across a period of years. Over and over, during that long stretched out process, I have remembered the words of India's poet, Rabindranath Tagore: "I have spent my life stringing and unstringing my instrument, and the song I came to sing remains unsung."[2]

I string and unstring no longer. Now—for you—I sing my song.

I

Leadership Can't Work Undefined

If you are a leader, exert yourself to lead.
Romans 12:8

I stared hard at my brother. The mahogany expanse of my desktop stretched between us like a chasm. We sat silent across it—a flat reddish-brown barrier of separation—our eyes locked.

Gray-green leather chairs cooled the warm woodgrain colors of the executive office suite; the long low credenza behind me glistened with collected objects of art; indirect light turned a wall of oriental draperies into white silver on rusty gold; the warm shaggy beige carpet cushioned the room and soaked up stray sounds; the great black couch stretched out between two heavy paneled doors behind us closed shut. They all framed the hardening chill of tension between us—two brothers miles apart across an office desk. No interior decorator could hide it . . . nor soften its pain.

Family businesses turn themselves into battlefields. Raw anguish. Undeclared war. The conflict of generations. Sibling rivalry. Oedipal struggle. Human depravity. Original sin. Power politics. Prodigal sons. Elder brothers. Over this burnished desktop—a gulf of polished wood—estrangement and alienation and hell.

Whose fault?

Nobody's fault . . . everybody's fault . . . in corporate microcosm, the human predicament . . . the mess we're in . . . the way things are.

The Family and the Fuss

To understand the scene, you meet:

(1) Dad. The patron of the clan. Silver-haired, short and stocky,

physically powerful, singlemindedly intense. The classic inner-directed American entrepreneur. Founder, chief stockholder, H.E.B. Food Stores' final word. From scratch he built his company, working no one so hard as himself. Texas hill country has produced its share of giants: John Garner of Uvalde, Admiral Nimitz of Fredericksburg, President Lyndon and Lady Bird Johnson, the Schreiners of sheep and wool fame, Hal Peterson memorialized by his hospital. I'd appreciate it if you didn't leave my Dad's name off that list.

(2) Mom. Social-servant extraordinary, forty years heading our H. E. Butt Foundation philanthropies. Board of Directors, Texas State System of Hospitals Mental Health and Mental Retardation, longer than any member in history—now in her third six-year term—not honorary but active. For her, hospitals exist only to serve patients.

(3) Bill and Eleanor Crook. Eleanor, my sister (middle child of three), married Bill Crook before his presidency of San Marcos Academy, his national directorship of Vista (the domestic Peace Corps), his ambassadorship to Australia under Lyndon Johnson, his own multiple business ventures, their three delightful children. In marrying a husband like Bill, lovely Eleanor also proved herself bright.

(4) Charles. Graduate, University of Pennsylvania's Wharton School of Business and Finance. Ten years my junior, five years younger than Eleanor. Charles is the urbane yachtsman, tennist, social civic political leader: a business and industrial power.

(5) Barbara Dan—wow what a wife—and me. Age: mid-forties. Twenty-some years married. Three prize children: tennis player Howard III, golfer Stephen, artist Deborah Dan.

Dad's vision for H.E.B. focused clearly on one point. He wanted both sons in the business, working hard, carrying the load. My brother presented no problem. From Charles's early years he envisioned himself the businessman. His temperament, his education, his sense of purpose all pointed him to the company. He finished college and hit H.E.B. like a tornado. His work schedule staggered you. His discipline and dedication inspired awe. He worked brilliantly, he worked aggressively, and he lived to work.

Charles's driving pace made me furious. I thought he was show-ing off for Dad. Not that I didn't work hard. I started in our business thirty-odd years ago in the old downtown store across from Day's Pharmacy in Harlingen. My age: nine. My job that first Saturday: carrying ten-pound bags of potatoes from the stock room in the back up to the produce department in front. The next Saturday they promoted me to stocking P. and G. and Crystal White bar soap—before the days of the detergent revolution. Our shelving then—bin type, bottom tilted out—seemed ultra-mod-ern. My goal was full shelves, ample stocks, happy customers. My means was the white grocery apron around my neck, twice too big. Folded over, tucked under, tied tight around my middle, it still came down to my shoes. By the time I turned twelve I qualified as a cashier, back in the days you had to memorize the prices to pass your checker's test. I first managed a store the summer after I was fifteen. I worked, all right. My fury with Charles boiled up, not because I wasn't hitting the ball, but because his singlemind-edness made my own work complications look so bad.

Profits or Pulpits?

For years I had been a two-headed monster vocationally. My career as a lay preacher began as a college student more than twenty-five years ago. I never felt I'd be a traditional clergyman. Before I came into the company, after a religion major alongside my business courses, I took a postgraduate year in theology. From the beginning I spent a third of my time in speaking engagements away from H.E.B. From Germany to Hawaii, across all denomina-tional lines, from college campuses to big citywide crusades, from churches to business conventions, I preached.

Billy Graham repeatedly urged me to leave the business and preach full time. He was a great booster. I was flattered. I remem-ber going to Florida in 1953 for a series of services sponsored by a large group of churches—held in the open-air bandshell on Biscayne Bay in Miami. Their Dade County publicity man rented huge billboards:

HEAR HOWARD BUTT
"America's Greatest Young Preacher."
Billy Graham

Billy's enthusiasm helped our crowds, puffed me up like a ruptured baloney, and added to his critics—the ones who claim he gets carried away.

In those years I had two father-figures: H. E. Butt and Billy Graham. Each one wanted me following his footsteps. Of the two, closer at home was Dad. He and I both thought I would follow him heading the company. Dad generously supported my preaching. His agreement and encouragement had been crucial ever since I made my decision in the late 1940s to come into the business, yet continue to preach.

"If it's what you want to do, son, I'll help you," he said. "Carrying both jobs, you'll have to work awfully hard. But if it's what you want, you can count on my support." He lived up to the deal; on me the pressures grew.

My ministry prospered. Laymen sharing their Christian faith rallied around me. The Layman's Leadership Institutes attracted a broad spectrum of prominent people from business and the professions. Responsibility for these Institutes fell on me. Christian Men Incorporated, an interdenominational laymen's organization, emerged around my leadership. Laity Lodge, at our H. E. Butt Foundation Camp in the Texas hill country, blossomed as a significant center in church renewal. My load piled up.

I had been Dad's second man in our company for fifteen years. I looked forward to running things myself. The responsibility of Merchandising Vice President put sales of several million dollars under my direction each week. Advertising in over fifty newspapers, big budgets in radio and television, pricing policies, promotional programs, meat, produce, groceries, private-label manufacturing, general merchandise (nonfoods), trading stamps—to appeal to Mrs. Consumer, the ultimate boss—all these I orchestrated. More than five thousand H.E.B. employees remind me how much fun you can have as the orchestra's conductor. Sometimes it's not the music so much as the power in your baton.

The God of the Last Half

Now you grasp our desktop drama. Between Charles and me a power struggle flared up over which one of us would run the company succeeding Dad. In that power struggle, I lost. And yet in losing, I won. I won because of the kind of person Charles is, and Dad. I won because our family is a family of Christian believers. I won by the death and resurrection of Jesus Christ. And I learned how Authority and Submission can open up new life for you.

As a student years ago I preached a sermon on "The God of the Last Half." I never knew it would be so appropriate for me. Our Baylor Bears, sparked by my preacher friend Jack Robinson, swept to the NCAA basketball playoffs in Madison Square Garden. Athletically my claim to fame is *I sat on the bench in Madison Square Garden.* That year those Bears became the basketball darlings of the nation. Why? They were a "last-half" team, a never-say-die, look-out-when-you-think-they're-beat, "come-back" team. Over and over, like jack-in-a-box cinderellas they folded, so it seemed, but they wouldn't stay down. Last-half ballclubs always capture your enthusiasm. Just when they look finished you see them get back up to win. Jesus Christ is like that . . . the God who turns things upside down. Just when you think he's finished—crucified, dead, and buried—suddenly it's Easter. He works in us the same way. Conflict between Charles and me was only the game's first half. Ten years ago our company's top echelon, for all its external strength, was a soggy mess. Every H.E.B. employee—whether he knew it or not—was affected. Charles unlocked a new era by illustrating this book's theme. Inspired by God, he asserted his leadership, he acted on his authority, he called for my submission. My brother became what he is—a velvet-covered brick.

In his mid-twenties, when I was about thirty-five, Charles let me know he planned to succeed Dad in the top spot. Years before, when he was in high school, I had assured him I envisioned him taking the company's lead. But the passing of time and my own grasp on power made that memory very dim. Now, sitting in my office, his words bombed me:

"Howard, what are your long-range plans?"

"I don't know," I said. "One day at a time."

"We've got to think about the future," he said, "and if I'm going to stay then I'm going to be in charge. Leadership can't work undefined."

I spat out my answer. If words could be flames, mine would have burned up that desktop.

"Well, I don't plan to leave."

Charles insisted on knowing precisely who was in command. He refused to work under a part-time brother as a boss. He demanded our company hierarchy be spelled out. If I had known then what I know today, if I had understood the Christian principles of organization, if I had believed the Bible about Authority and Submission, I could have saved myself and everybody involved lots of pain. As it was I learned my lessons, but only just in time. Our company might lie in shambles today. Instead it thrives as never before. Charles was right, I was wrong in that scene so long ago.

Ten years my junior! That's what got me! Yet across my desk you'd never have known it. Charles made like a rock—color him granite—the epitome of unflappable poise. Yes, a brick. You cannot push around a brick. It sits firm, secure, steady. A leader asserting his leadership; a man who knows his authority. That kind of God-given authority can naturally be gentle. Can naturally be tender. Kind. Patient. Loving. And yet . . . unshakable. A brick. A velvet-covered brick.

I reacted so furiously to Charles's proposal that Dad seemed stunned. Next to myself, I felt sorriest for Dad. Fathers helping sons grow up spiritually—not just physically—chiefly get to suffer. Charles and I learned about velvet-covered bricks first from Dad. The Father in heaven—cosmic leadership—gives us lessons through our fathers on earth.

The Kingdom with Keys

Our family crisis turned on one dramatic pivot. My oldest son, Howard (H.E.B. III), is an outstanding athlete, a Texas Boys

Tennis Champion, long, tall, as strong as blue steel. Even though tennis is my game he began beating me by the time he was twelve. I was raised on a sports diet of wrestling with Dad. But Howard and I kept our contests on the court; we never wrestled each other or physically fought.

One Sunday night during our corporate storm, young Howard and I broke the pattern: we got into a fight. At first it was playful. But the more we threw each other across our bedroom and its furniture, the less we laughed. Howard's younger brother, Stephen, and little Debbie shrieked and screamed us on. Barbara Dan rode it out in the womb of her warm bathtub. Not a crack in her door as around her dressing room crashed thunder and lightning. The first fifteen minutes I kept thinking any moment I'd have him down. I outweighed him twenty-five pounds. Though my headlock kept him hurting, I couldn't pin him to the floor. The last fifteen minutes both my mood and my strength ran down. My doubts overwhelmed me. Turning weaker by the second, panting, struggling, gasping for a good mouthful of air, I grunted an ignominious retreat.

"Okay, Buddy. Let's call it a tie."

In mercy he accepted. As I got up to stare at my purple-faced humiliation in the mirror I saw how our sweat had soaked the imported carpet. I should have quit sooner just to protect the house.

Later that evening over cookies in the kitchen Stephen and Debbie watched young Howard and me as we rehashed the battle.

"Pal," I said, "you are some terrific fighter. I've learned my lesson. Let's make a deal."

"Okay," he said.

"Let's never fight each other again. I'll be on your side. Or you be on mine."

"Okay, Dad," he said. "It's a deal."

The next morning I was up early, getting ready for work. I use this time consciously to commit the day to God. Organizing your own individual worship is absolutely personal, the core of all privacy. Jesus said, "Enter your closet and shut the door."[1] I was bathing and dressing to go to the office. As the hot shower bombarded me, I was praying. I gave thanks for Christ's victory: (1)

over *the world* around us; (2) over *the flesh* within us; (3) over *the Devil* who attacks us.

I thought the night before was forgotten. I was praying about the day ahead. But right there—right in the middle of a shower on my aching back—I got devotionally stuck. I found myself reviewing the strategy of Satan to destroy God and humanity. We had just been studying the fifth chapter of Ephesians about Christian interpersonal relationships: "Submit yourselves to one another in the fear of God."[2]

The Bible principle stood vivid in my mind that morning: husband, head of the wife; wife to be submissive. Parents, leaders in the home; children to be submissive. Employers, leaders on the job; employees to be submissive. It got me! My father is my employer! God commands my submissiveness!

I had been stabbed with light . . . an overwhelming insight, a ponderous view of my shame. Years before, facts had forced me to acknowledge a profound guilt in my attitude toward Dad as a son. I had unconsciously allowed my religious work to become a way to compete with my father. He was a successful businessman; I'd be an even more successful lay preacher. Now the obvious concomitant faced me: I had also competed with Dad in the very business he founded for us. My inward resistance to Dad's opinions and desires; my irritation with his old-fogey conservatism, my conviction I could run the company better than he was running it; my resentment of his authority, his decisions, his leadership, his control—these attitudes came tumbling into my mind, revealed naked by the truth. Rebellion against authority is rebellion against God. In all this competitive rivalry I was expressing toward my Dad the hellish opposite of love. My lack of submission revealed my desperate spiritual need. Satan originally rebelled against God's sovereign authority; revolt stays demonic; in my rebellion against the authority of my boss I join forces with Satan.

While I dressed I continued to pray. I turned my failure to love —my sin of disorder—over to Christ. I gave thanks for the victory he won for us through his death and resurrection. I claimed its gift for myself for that day. I had been drawn to an important new step; that much seemed clear. What next?

At breakfast I shared with Barbara Dan my new insight.

"This morning," I said, "when I get to the office I'm going to tell Dad I owe him an apology."

She listened thoughtfully, frowning.

"I'll tell him from now on, as far as I'm concerned, he'll be the boss."

Barbara Dan knew such a conversation right then would be loaded. I had pleaded with Dad to "get Charlie's attitude straightened out." He was refusing. He kept saying, "You and Charles have got to work things out between yourselves." Barbara Dan knew: submitting to Dad meant submitting to Charles. My wife was my fiercest protagonist.

"Don't be in a hurry" was all she said.

Before the day was out I had my conversation with Dad. I told him I had wrestled him long enough. As I gave him my regret, my apology, my confession, his face warmed into a smile.

The agreement Charles and I worked out eventually was hardest on Dad. Charles got what he wanted—leadership in the company made clear. I got what I wanted—freedom to concentrate on my ministries outside. But Dad was called on to adjust—to submit—to my absence in the company's day-to-day affairs.

A family mess turned into a family miracle. Authority exercised, submission accepted: the secret of social order. "Submitting yourselves to one another in the fear of God" is the organizational how-to of Christian love. The Kingdom of God is a kingdom with keys. Leadership and Submission are two sides of the same coin, two edges on the same key. Charles's submission to God produced his courage, standing up asserting his leadership. Out of submission flows authority. Rebellion is the shortsighted route to progress. When people on the bottom in any group or society want to revolt, people on the top grow increasingly repressive. When people on the top get repressive, people on the bottom more and more want revolution. Repression and rebellion feed each other—the meal they eat is fear. Christ's broken body destroyed that cycle of organizational despair. The meal he serves is love. The successor to rebellion is submission. Revolution went out of date at Christ's cross. "Under Pontius Pilate" he suffered. Rather than revolt, he died. Submission for him meant death. Resurrection revealed him: the Velvet Covered Brick. "All authority is given to me," he said. "Go and make disciples."[3] Christ came to introduce a new kind of authority. The crisis of our age is the authority crisis. Eric Hoffer says the battle between communism and capitalism is fundamentally a battle between bosses.[4] Shiny desktops yawn wide into chasms of estrangement between us. Rough wood, sharp splinters, and the old rugged cross mean that all our organizational gulfs have been bridged.

II

The Style of the Servant-King

Think as Christ Jesus thought. . . .
Philippians 2:5

This is the story of two men, a book, and a telephone.

The book was written by the first man, Chester Barnard. He named it *The Functions of the Executive*. Harvard University Press published it first in 1938. It is a classic among men who specialize in management. Barnard says that problems in organization seldom come from "the excessive desire of individuals to assume responsibility." Just the contrary. The difficulties spring from "their reluctance to *take* responsibility."[1] "Executives frequently fail, . . ." he says, "resulting in the *destruction of responsibility.*"[2] Barnard was president of the Bell Telephone Company of New Jersey. "Executive responsibility" is his name for leadership.

Our second man is different.

Donn Moomaw was U.C.L.A.'s great linebacker, three times All-American. Instead of professional football he decided on the Presbyterian ministry. He went for training to New Jersey, to Princeton Seminary. Shortly before finishing, he got his first job offer. Robert Boyd Munger, senior minister at Berkeley's First Presbyterian Church, wanted him back in California on his staff. It was a hard decision for Moomaw. Would he fit? How could he know? Was he ready to settle down? He could not decide. His unsureness grew. He became distraught. He called California. Long distance. New Jersey Bell. Pay phone. Dormitory hall. Chester Barnard never knew the drama on his phone, but it threw new light on his book. Drained by his final exams, disheveled by his uncertainity, Moomaw grasped the phone. Placed the call. Stood waiting. Munger answered. The young preacher poured out to the older one his torrent of apologies. His indecision embarrassed him. He felt guilty about the delay. Why should he be so upset?

The telephone caught his agitation.

Bob Munger's voice stayed calm.

"Of course, Donn, I understand. Don't worry. God assumes the responsibility."

God assumes the responsibility.

Later, Moomaw wound up going to Berkeley. Do you wonder? God assumes the responsibility.

Why do you love Jesus Christ? Why do you cherish his leadership? Because he took responsibility for the world. Barnard says the highest expression of executive responsibility is moral creativeness. Christ's cross is the ultimate moral creativity. His resurrection is responsibility indestructible. Think of God as "the Responsible Executive."

The Only Thing That Ever Really Happened: Christ's Past

In *Dr. Zhivago*, Boris Pasternak wrote: "Rome was a flea market of borrowed gods and conquered peoples, a bargain basement on two floors, earth and heaven, a mass of filth convoluted in a triple knot as in an intestinal obstruction. . . . Eyes sunk in fat, sodomy, double chins, illiterate emperors, fish fed on the flesh of learned slaves. . . . All wretched. And then, into this tasteless heap of gold and marble . . . He came. Light—and clothed in an aura. Emphatically human, deliberately provincial, Galilean. . . . At that moment gods and nations ceased to be and Man came into being. . . ."[3]

You can't think of God ever again as a great gray blob. Jesus of Nazareth was so blessedly specific: "When Herod was King of Judea . . . a decree from Caesar Augustus . . . when Cyrenius was governor of Syria. . . ."[4] As if I were to say: "When Richard Nixon was president, more precisely while Preston Smith was governor of Texas, in particular when Ronnie Sizemore was mayor of Corpus Christi, this, this, and this happened." It would be hard for you to get confused.

What happened?

History's premier people, out of their own land of Israel, produced more than they themselves had come to expect. They produced a Messiah not for themselves alone but for the whole human race. The details overpower us. One particular man in one particular time in one particular place claimed to be God. He claimed universal presence: "Where two or three are gathered in my name there am I in the midst of them."[5] He claimed to fill all human desires: "I am the bread of life; he who comes to me shall not hunger."[6] He claimed to embody all strength and wisdom: "I am the way, the truth, and the life."[7] He claimed timelessness: "Before Abraham was, I am."[8] He claimed power over death: "He that believes in me shall never die."[9] He claimed potential human liberation: "If the Son shall make you free you shall be free indeed."[10] He claimed unconditional availability: "Come unto me, all you who labor and are heavy laden and I will give you rest."[11] What do you make of a man who talks this way? The first person pronouns: "I, I, I, me, me, I, I,". . . constantly he speaks of himself . . . yet his listeners believe he is Humility? Jesus of Nazareth claimed to be God.

Can you read the record and rationally believe he was only a man, just a great teacher, a man and nothing more? No, you cannot. You would ignore the account, blind yourself to evidence, violate a coherent use of words. If he was only a man then he was not good. C. S. Lewis said that to explain Jesus as a great teacher is the one option he did not leave us. He did not intend to. When a man claims to be God how do you react? You have only three choices:

(1) You can believe he is insane: on a level with someone who claims he is a poached egg. Asylums give you lots of data on people who think they are Stalin or Churchill or Roosevelt or God.

(2) You can believe he is a demon: he claims deity to exploit gullible victims. He is a fraud, an impostor, a charlatan, a deceiver, or worse.

(3) You can believe he is what he says: God.[12]

You have no other credible choice before you, no possible alternative. The religious leaders of Jesus' day at least had intellectual integrity. They paid their money, took their choice, and picked Choice Number Two. Proceeding logically from their conclusion, they elected to kill him. History questions their judgment: if you ever saw sanity, if you ever saw goodness it was in this man. We are drawn irresistibly to Choice Number Three. Jesus of Nazareth, joltingly historic, was God in human flesh. God with name, rank, and serial number. Bethlehem: God's Normandy, the penetration point where his invasion broke through. The beachhead for a new humanity was a baby's body, twenty inches long. The God of the telescope, author of incomprehensible vastnesses in cosmic space; the God of the microscope, architect of infinitesimal blueprints in atomic structure: this God had now appeared on earth in person —a baby in a barn.

Two miracles in one: God stooping to become man; man exalted to become God. He was the God-man. No, that overemphasizes one. He was the man-God. No, that overemphasizes the other. Say it faster then . . . God-man, man-God. I can't do it, I can't say them both simultaneously. Absolute man, as if he had not been God. Absolute God, as if he had not been man. Perfect man: perfect God. Son of man—representative humanity. Son of God—representative deity. The Almighty compacted down into one living, breathing, growing human.

God stood six-foot-three.

God had brown hair.

God weighed 185 pounds.

I don't know his weight, his coloring, his height. The point is, he was a specific identifiable man. Jesus Christ was older than his mother. When the Virgin Mary supernaturally gave birth to Jesus, she gave birth to a body, but the personality had been existing forever, for the personality was the personality of God. He made the ground she walked on. He made the air she breathed. He made the water she drank. "All things were made by him."[13] He was older than his mother. "In the beginning was the Word," says John's Gospel, "and the Word was with God and the Word was God . . . and the Word became flesh."[14] "Incarnation" is the theologian's capsule-word. "Incarnation" has a graphic base: *carne*, meat, flesh, as in our chili-con-carne. *Incarnation:* en-

fleshed, you see God. You, today: are you tired? God understands
that; he got tired too. Do you feel weak? He did too; he needed
rest. Do you get tempted? He waded through every human temptation. Have your friends let you down? His did. One of them
betrayed him. Have you got problems with your family? So did he.
Are you lonely? His God-forsaken cross was lonelier still. Does
guilt bother you? To fully taste our guilt, he died. He understands
your problem: he has been through it himself.

He died for you.

The blood he shed for you—his life outpoured—was human
blood like yours.

Three days later he was alive again—really alive—as you cannot
be without him.

The resurrection of Jesus of Nazareth stands today the most
validly authenticated fact of ancient history. If you have trouble
believing it, as I once did, read—for yourself—the accounts in the
Bible. You also might want to read Frank Morrison's *Who Moved
the Stone?* Morrison started to write a book *disproving* the resurrection but could not make the facts fit. His book reads like a
detective story. You become interested in Christ's future after you
are gripped by his past.

Becoming What We Will Be: Christ's Future

The death and resurrection of Christ give you your keys for
tomorrow: the cross as submission; the resurrection as authority.
"Jesus Christ the same yesterday, today, and forever."[15] In submission and authority you see the Everlasting Always.

> Beyond the sunset is tomorrow's wisdom,
> Today will be long, long ago.[16]

Tomorrow's wisdom about authority and submission gives you
Christian hope today. Christianity is leadership-training: you become a leader. History's most spectacular course in leader-develop-
ment was Christ getting his twelve original men trained. Nothing
else in educational annals even comes close. Beside it, Socrates and
his pupils look like raw green amateurs. Christ turned straw into

bricks, nobodies into somebodies, recruits into generals. They were ordinary-run-of-the-mill-picked-up-off-the-street-who-ever-heard-of-them-nonentities. But they spun their generation around 180 degrees.

Why?

Simple.

They expected Christ to come back. Christ's return to rule meant they were rulers too. Their prospect determined their posture. Their hope described their habits. The promise of rule to come—future tense—gave them, then and there, a present-tense psychology of leadership. Twenty centuries later, I expect Christ's return too. That hope once more again today makes me a leader. I am ruling with Christ already now. In my home, on my job, wherever I am called by God to lead, Christ makes me a responsible executive. Maybe you call that corny. Cornball religion, backwoods theology, hayseed hermeneutics, country music, the Nashville sound, and HEE HAW. We traded *in* red-hot eschatology. We preferred red-hot politics. But our trade isn't working out. Now politics hands us back Armageddon.

Christ—the King who is coming—gives his Kingdom to you now.

"As my Father has given me the right to rule," he said, "so I will make the same agreement with you. . . ."[17]

"In union with Christ Jesus he raised us up to rule with him."[18]

"You have made them a Kingdom of priests to serve our God; and they shall rule on earth."[19]

Do you realize how incalculably important this is to you? In whatever place of authority you serve you have divine backing. Jesus Christ, resurrected from the dead, alive forevermore, is reigning now as the King in his Kingdom. "For he must continue to be King until he puts all his enemies under his feet."[20] He in us; us in him: ruling. Under Christ every Christian is a king, confident in his appointed leadership. "The Church also shares the prerogative of their King," says George Eldon Ladd. "They are granted the right to rule with Christ. They are a Kingdom, a nation of kings."[21]

"But, Howard," you say, "has the Kingdom come yet?"

Yes and No. It *has* come; it *is* coming; it *will* come. From God's viewpoint each tense (or time) inheres in the others: in Christ the Kingdom *has* come. From *our* viewpoint the Kingdom has not yet come fully. It awaits our Lord's return; it awaits consummation.

"Then are we kings already?"

Yes . . . you are a king now as surely as Jesus Christ is a King now. Believe it and give thanks. Don't be afraid of leadership's *raison d'être*, its rational support, its ground of being. Christ is reigning now—awaiting only his denouement, his disclosure, his revelation. "As he is, so are we in the world."[22]

"Let no man rob you of your crown."[23]

Our generation falls apart without this kind of good news. Where do we get a doctrine of leadership, of organization, of authority? Our modern dilemmas all point us to sickness in structures, institutions, organizations: families, schools, corporations, communes, governments. Every utopia founders in bureaucracy. Every leader fights against disorder. Communists call it revision, capitalists call it protest. Both suffer the same disease: authority divorced from equality.

Human equality has been man's dream forever. Two hundred years ago Jean-Jacques Rousseau distilled a philosophy of politics out of pure equality. It formed the French Revolution's core: *"Liberté, Egalité, Fraternité."* It did not work. "Pure equality" in 1789 was followed in 1799 by Napoleon. *Can* you combine both equality and order? Leadership alone gives you tyranny—a dictator trampling inconsequential nobodies. Equality alone gives you anarchy—a headless crowd of uncoordinated rebels. Could you *merge* leadership and equality? Could you save both and not lose either? Could you have hierarchy among equals?

Women's lib, school busing, the third world—we struggle with equality like a porcupine. All our agonizing crises—the young, the black, the poor—haunt us as failures in leadership. How do you fuse leadership and equality? You look at God, that's how—at the true and living God, the God who is composite unification, the God who, himself, is Triunity. Christians believe God is organizational perfection. Love is unified: the doctrine of Trinity. God is

Three—Father, Son, Holy Spirit—yet One. The best in human organizations flows from this Triunity in God. Differences are not divisions; differentiation demands coordination. God is love and love is organized. Perfect individuality could never conflict with perfect unitedness. The single individual is never divorced from the community group: the One, Triune. Perfect love is perfect organization: Three in One. Triunity pivots on submission.

Christ's inner personality strikes at the root of your submissiveness fears. Submission does not demean you. It is not low and ignoble and groveling. It is high and holy and exalting. The only way you become Christlike is to yield, to surrender, to submit. Why? Because the life within God himself is authority and submission: One in Three; Three in One. Father means authority. Son means submission. Father means above. Son means below. Jesus teaches us authority when we pray, "Our Father who art in heaven."[24] He teaches us submission by calling himself "Son of God" and "Son of man." The Father over the Son; the Son under the Father: Deity is organized; hierarchy among equals.

Christianity teaches us a hierarchy of function but not of value. Christ did not count his equality with God something to be clutched at or grasped or hoarded. "Though the divine nature was his from the first, he humbled himself and became a man."[25] In value was Christ less than God? In value was the Son below the Father? Of course not: the Scriptures stand crystal clear. Church history confirmed them in A.D. 325. Athanasius the trinitarian saint triumphed over Arius the unitarian heretic. In value Christ the eternal Son and God the eternal Father stand forever equal. Secure in his equal value, Christ humbled himself to become a man: the Father above the Son, the Son below the Father *in function.*

And that, ladies and gentlemen, is the key to the organizational atom, $E = MC^2$, for any human group, for all human order. Hierarchy in function depends on equality in value. When I am secure in my value as your equal, I can accept inequality beneath you as my role.

I become the supporter of your hierarchy. I am not afraid to submit. And neither are you. Health produces submission and submission produces leadership. Without this lesson we rule out human community. Submission steps down to lift authority up. Community rests on the nature of the Triune God. Equal Worth: Different Roles.

God the Father as Divine Authority.

Christ the Son as Human Limitation.

The Holy Spirit: God too big to be boxed.

Human figures like father and son burst open within God who is a Spirit. "The words 'God is love' have no real meaning unless God contains at least two persons," said C. S. Lewis. "Love is something that one person has for another person. If God was a single person, then before the world was made, He was not love."[26] How then will we love each other? Like God: organization. Authority and submission. Fathers and sons, husbands and wives. Parents and children. Hierarchy and support. God is an envelope of organization and the community inside is love.

Christ's return is our hope—now as well as later. You see yourself already as a responsible executive, a velvet-covered brick, a king in submissive authority. Now. "Hope deferred makes the heart sick," said King Solomon.[27] Don't defer your hope . . . use it. Responsible leadership blossoms in hope, withers in hopelessness. "Hopelessness can assume two forms," says Jürgen Moltmann: "presumption and despair. . . . Presumption is a premature, selfwilled anticipation of the fulfillment of what we hope for from God. Despair is a premature, arbitrary anticipation of the nonfulfillment of what we hope for from God."[28] *Presumption clutches for leadership too fast. Despair shrinks from leadership it already has.*

I cannot tell you *all* that the second coming of Christ will mean. But of one thing I am sure. Here and now it means a new kind of Christian leadership. The Christ to come is the Christ within you. Christ's Everlasting Always draws you to the Everlasting Now.

Teaching Us to Lead: Christ's Present

The keynote of Christ's first coming was submission. His second coming will be keynoted by authority. "This very same Jesus will come. . . ."[29] This very same King in this very same Kingdom. . . . You cannot escape the King.

In 1743 London heard its first performance of George Frederick Handel's new oratorio, *Messiah*. England's reigning monarch George II inspired history as the singers reached the climactic "Hallelujah Chorus". Reverently, quietly, the king rose to his feet.

"King of kings and Lord of lords . . . and He shall reign forever."

Centuries before, to the cacophony of a howling mob, another ruler, Pontius Pilate, nailed a sign above a cross:

"Jesus of Nazareth, King of the Jews."[30]

In three languages he wrote it. In Hebrew, the language of religion; in Latin, the language of government; in Greek, the language of culture.[31] In the three universal languages: "This is Jesus the King!" A mocking political joke. A scrawny sign above a scrawny cross. A routine execution outside a city garbage dump. Today the human race cannot forget that sign. Why? You know why.

Jesus was a Servant-King.

Kings there had been aplenty. From Tammuz, Gilgamesh, and Sargon of the Sumerians to Hammurabi, king of Babylon. From Thutmose, Amenhotep, and Ramses of the Egyptians to Ashurbanipal, king of Assyria. From Cyrus, Darius, and Xerxes of the Persians to Alexander the Great of Greece. Numberless they came and went. Kings aplenty there had been.

But never a Servant-King.

Civilization's earliest kingships, historians tell us, combined the offices of warrior, priest, and father.[32] Later the king became lawgiver, ruler, and judge. But *servant?* Did you say "servant"?

Servant.

The Servant-King.

Have you looked at Jesus fulfilling Hebrew prophecy? The signposts are innumerable. The specifics jolt you. God's leadership— rejected—brought the prophet Micah to write, "You, Bethlehem, from you shall he come forth to rule . . . whose origin is of old."[33] Seven centuries later he was born in Bethlehem. And leadership —corrupted—caused the prophet Zechariah to write, "They weighed for my price thirty pieces of silver."[34] Five centuries later Judas sold Christ for thirty silver pieces, the price of a Hebrew slave. But nowhere does Hebrew prophecy grip you more than in

Isaiah's Servant Song: "I was not rebellious. . . . I gave my back to the smiters and my cheeks to those who pulled out the beard. I hid not my face from shame and spitting . . . despised, rejected by man . . . man of sorrows . . . bruised for our iniquities. . . . Your God has become your King. . . . Behold, my servant shall prosper, he shall be exalted . . . lifted up . . . very high . . . so shall he startle many nations."[35] Seven centuries after Isaiah spoke, Christ walked the long dusty road to Calvary—into the jaws of death, into the mouth of hell—and out on the other side. The Deliverer King is the Suffering Servant.

What is Christ doing now? His past is the key to his present. He is doing what he did in the days of his flesh. He is calling out a people for his name. Out of every race and tribe and nation, he is drawing to himself his larger organization.

How is he doing it?

By his Spirit.

After the resurrection Jesus told his followers to wait in Jerusalem. Several weeks went by. Then came the Jewish holiday called Pentecost. The Church had arrived at Normandy—its own Bethlehem. Many people saw Jesus physically after his resurrection. Paul says over five hundred at one time. But how could he keep his promise of universal presence? How could he stay available to us all? Limited to his physical body he could not. So he left physically but sent us his Spirit. The Spirit is the living Jesus with us now. He is Christ universalized. Through the Spirit Jesus can be in Jerusalem, Cairo, New York, and San Francisco simultaneously. He can be with you there and me here, both. Jesus spoke of the Holy Spirit as another Comforter, Counselor, Encourager like himself. The Spirit throws his spotlight on Christ. "When he comes," said Jesus, "he shall glorify me."[36] How did you first believe in Christ? By the Holy Spirit. "Whoever does not have the Spirit of Christ does not belong to him."[37] The Spirit lives within every Christian. He makes Christ real to you. He reproduces Christ's life in you. He shapes us as the Church, Christ's body. By the Spirit we become parts, organs, members of Christ in the contemporary world. Christ, the head of the Church—its executive director—is at work within us now. Your head, your brain, your nervous system controls your physical body. Christ's body depends on the Holy Spirit; the Trinity is interdependence. God is an organizational Spirit; he organizes the organism. He carries out in every finger and toe the central ruling thought of the Head. So now Christ's Spirit is producing Christ's life again, in us. We are becoming little Christs. We are becoming servant-kings. We are becoming the true Church.

It isn't easy.

Back in 1950 some young boys in New York got themselves a good thing going. It was during the peak months *South Pacific* played on Broadway. Rodgers and Hammerstein had hatched a big hit, Ezio Pinza was singing to Mary Martin and sellout crowds, and lots of visitors from out in the boondocks way up there in the big city wanted to see the show but . . . not a chance. Not near enough tickets. Rural America got crowded out. So these enterprising young New Yorkers—always alert—picked up dropped ticket stubs and thrown-down programs from the sidewalks in front of the theater. And then they sold them to hicks from the sticks like us! Sooo . . . we buy a used program and a ticket stub and we come back home to our friends. Our first evening with these local yokels wallowing in their cultural deprivation, fingering our ticket stubs, we cannot resist the temptation to tune-drop. Very quietly, starting in a nasal hum:

> Some enchanted eefning,
> You may see a stranjurr.
> You may see a stranjurr.
> A-cross zee crowded room. . . .

Ezio Pinza, in cowboy boots. We've got words, music, tickets, program, everything. There is only one hitch. We haven't seen the show.

And that, I am sorry to say, is a parable of the Church. We have the tickets—members in good standing. We have the program— Holy Bible, gathering dust. We have the songs—passionate hymns, half embarrassing. There is only one minor fraud. We have not seen the show for ourselves. "Hearsay Christianity" has vaccinated us against the genuine article. Sam Shoemaker asks us all: "What has Jesus Christ meant to you since 7 o'clock this morning? Is your Christianity ancient history or current events?" Every Christian is a miniature Christ made modern. Past-tense religion is a denial of the resurrection. God's name is *I AM*, not *I WAS*.

Can you go from hearsay yesterday to attestation today? Can somebody else's secondhand religion turn into your very own firsthand reality? Can Christ's resurrection become neither myth nor memory but experience for you to taste? How do you get there? What is the route?

Problems

Conflicts

Trouble

Pain

Organizational Estrangement

Hangups & Breakdowns

War

Agony

Tyranny

Tragedy

Sufferings

Revolution

My word-form makes you a picture. Resurrections only follow crucifixions. Everyone faces the harshnesses I list. Everyone tastes their acid. Everyone dreads their hurt. But only Christ knows their potential . . . nailed to a cross.

God calls us in the language we understand best . . . our circumstances . . . the mess we're in . . . our ordinary everyday problems. My problems become the divinely ordained route to the end of my rope. Only at the end of my rope can I make contact with God. A Christian is a man who has come to the end of his rope; a mature Christian is one who lives at the end of his rope all day, every day. "The peace of man is freedom from adversity. The peace of God is freedom from self."[38]

You notice that the cross-bar in our picture, the horizontal arm, is formed by "Organizational Estrangements, Hangups & Breakdowns." Why did I show it that way? Not only because it's our theme. Far more, it describes the central torture of our era. It affects all of us personally—in our families.

Do you remember *The Peter Principle?* Lawrence Peter and Raymond Hull wrote a secular book of Christian comedy—about hierarchies. They defined their terms: a hierarchy is "any organization whose members or employees are arranged in order of rank, grade, or class." And they gave us their now famous principle: "In a Hierarchy Every Employee Tends to Rise To His Level of Incompetence." All our common pesky pedestrian problems made their tongue-in-cheek study hilarious. From the roof-glare in Houston's Astrodome to the rattles in Detroit's cars, all around us is "incompetence rampant, incompetence triumphant."[39]

But if you think about it awhile your laughter turns to tears. I rose to my own incompetence level above my wife when I got married. When babies started coming our household hierarchy showed more strain. And ever since . . . for instance, this past week. . . .

Several evenings ago Barbara Dan served as stand-in for us both at Stephen's school. "Parents' Night" they called it. At our house it lived up to the name. I had begged off from the activities at the school to stay home. I needed to work on this writing. Also to look after Debbie, our ten-year-old. Before my wife drove off I got her schedule refresher:

"And don't forget bedtime for Debbie. Nine o'clock, nine-thirty at the latest."

"Don't worry," I said.

In charge, that's me: the hierarch on duty. When I grew up, O.D. didn't mean overdose, it meant Officer of the Day. I was Parent of the Night.

What happened?

I'm ashamed to tell you.

I forgot Debbie. Got engrossed in my work. Ignored my daughter.

Barbara Dan came home—10:30 or a little past. Down the hall I heard her coming. At Debbie's room she stopped. Stepped in. Our ten-year-old tornado was still going strong. Thriving on her late-night dissipation. My wife blew up. She jumped me. I jumped Debbie. Heaven help the cat. I spare you the grisly details. We looked like a Christian family washout. And I don't mean Debbie's tears.

It was bad . . . very bad. Me and my compulsive habits of work! I was the executive irresponsible, the hierarchy incompetent, the king absentee. If God can save me he can save anybody. Leadership in the family, school, shop, town, nation: in all of them Christ nails us. He calls us to something new, the most radical idea about leadership ever heard:

"Whoever wants to be first must place himself last of all."

"The leader must be like the servant."

"I am among you as One Who Serves."[40]

What does that mean? I call it The Pastor Principle: *"Organizations demand leaders. Leaders do not lead to lead; leaders lead to serve. They serve by leading; they lead by serving. In the Spirit of the Father and the Son. Amen."*

I am glad to tell you our "Parents' Night" conclusion. I committed my sin to Christ. I thanked him for his death and resurrection . . . my forgiveness and my victory. I apologized to the ladies. On my compulsive work problem I enlisted the whole family's help. They agreed: I need it. But how else could writing this book not become a literary screen, a wall of family alienation? And already this week my self-control on work habits is improving.

What is taking place?

(1) *I am experiencing Christ-in-me.* My old self, estranged from God and people, has been counted dead with Christ. My self, my work, my book have got dethroned. Christ has been enthroned in me again. Reality has been recognized: Christ reigns. Christ-in-me, as my goodness, frees me to admit my own badness. Another thin layer of irresponsibility drops away. I take one more step toward the life of the responsible executive, the competent hierarch, the servant-king.

(2) *I am experiencing Christ-in-the-Church.* Barbara Dan did us all a favor by getting angry. The Bible says, "Be angry and sin not."[41] I needed her honest feelings. My family "speaks the truth in love" calling on me to submit.[42] As ministers of God: as prophets, priests, and kings they help me change. This house where I am living becomes a residential unit of the larger Church.

Tomorrow will bring new problems. New challenges in leadership and in submission. How will I react? I do not know. But I can count on Christ's sure dependability. The Christian life is not difficult . . . it is impossible. I can't live it; I am never surprised when I fail. But Christ is living it now for us all, unfailingly. He offers to live his life in me.

III

Love: Authority That Wins

Let no one rob you of your crown.
Revelation 3:11

"Organization is a moral problem" says management specialist Robert Golembiewski.[1] *Men, Management, and Morality* he called his book. I write for you about Joe Christian the manager, the father, the president, the leader. In the first two chapters I introduced you to authority and submission in my own experience and in the originating source. In these next two chapters, first from the authority view on top, then from the submissiveness view below, we look at the problem of our organizational morality and its solution.

Morality begins at the top: moral leaders produce moral organizations; immoral organizations come from leaders who are immoral. Nazi parties come from Adolf Hitlers. Your only alternative to organizational tyranny is the organizational God: Father means leader; Son means follower. Since the Father and the Son are indivisible—we worship One God, not three—you can't split authority and submission. You can't think of God *except* as a servant. Authority and submission interlock constantly; they interact flexibly. Who is the Christ within you? "In Him dwells all the fullness of the Godhead bodily."[2] In you: the Spirit of the Father and of the Son, both. God the leader and God the follower mesh in Christ to produce within you his moral originality. The word "gospel" means "good news" not only for individuals, but also for organizations and institutions and governments.

Pessimism about organizations—from the family to bureaucracies—shrouds us in despair. Who is to blame? We are: the men on top, the establishment, the leaders. *New York Times* education editor Fred Hechinger reports:

Shortly after the by now all but forgotten uprising at Columbia University, a group of moderately radical students organized a postmortem weekend at Arden House to which they invited a variety of higher education experts. During one of the sessions one university president gave an eloquent account of the academy's many deficiencies and an even more eloquent description of the snail's pace of educational reforms. When he sat down, a bearded and obviously angry young man jumped to his feet. "What I want to know is who the hell is in charge?" he shouted.

The question came as a surprise to university administrators who had been fearful of being typecast in the role of autocrats. Yet the radical student appeared to be complaining not of autocracy but of the absence of campus leadership. He had accurately diagnosed the most serious deficiency of higher education: No one, in fact, was in charge.

The leadership crisis, far from being unique to the campus, is part of the more general drift. The absence of resolute leadership seems endemic to the times. It is not evidence of strong and purposeful leadership when industrial empires such as Lockheed Aircraft or Penn Central gradually drift into expensive bankruptcies, when the railroads chug along on a steady journey to suicide. . . . Leadership has been given a bad name by its perversion in dictatorships. But the strong men of totalitarianism were the final outcome of an extreme reaction to the absence of legitimate leaders.[3]

Moral bankruptcy now brings us to a bankruptcy of our institutions—which comes first, diseased chickens or rotten eggs?—institutional collapse producing the collapse of morality. Some argue the virtues of anarchy, others call for leadership's destruction. Open season on authority. "Leaderless groups" emerge as a fad. "Pure equality" threatens the nation. *Leaderless groups?* Bosh. The real leadership is either confused or hidden . . . or else the group is breaking apart. *Leaderless groups* are unanalyzed groups: temporary, superficial, synthetic. *Leaderless groups* prove psychological unrealities, social impossibilities, practical monstrosities. Every group develops its own leadership; leadership is the law of the group; without leadership you have no group. Leadership is linkage: without fatherhood you lose brotherhood.

Leadership theology: Jesus was, is, and continues to produce a leadership of love. Agape authority offers you both (1) freedom and (2) organization. Where else can you get both? Christ talked organizational language—about students and teachers, caretakers and owners, servants and masters, children and parents, subjects and kingdoms, sons and fathers. The early church understood. They talked organizational language too: "Bosses, remember you have a Boss in heaven. He makes no distinctions between boss and employee."[4] What were they saying? Precisely what they found their Lord to *be*. Hierarchy united with equality: the leader and the led as equals.

Aristippus, the Greek philosopher, was asking a favor of Dionysius, ruler of the city of Syracuse. Repeatedly the king ignored him. Finally, tired of getting no attention, Aristippus fell down before the royal feet. Dionysius stopped, listened, and granted the philosopher his request. Later someone jealous for the reputation of philosophy scolded Aristippus for subjecting the profession of philosophy to such an indignity. For a purely personal favor he had fallen down before the feet of a tyrant. Aristippus replied: "It was not my fault but the fault of Dionysius. He has his ears in his feet."

Eyeball to eyeball or ears in your feet: two different kinds of leadership. Dionysian theology or Christ's? "The man who stresses his downward authority," says famed consultant Peter Drucker, "is a subordinate no matter how exalted his title and rank. But the man who focuses on contribution (serving) and who takes responsibility for results (leading), no matter how junior, is in the most literal sense 'top management.' "[5] Servant kings, responsible executives. Management books (the good ones) think God's thoughts after him. Or you can go straight to the Author. We hear lots today about "participative management." *Time* magazine says "the ideas are so new that only a handful of companies have tried them."[6] Of course. The ideas are as new as the Bible.

How can I test myself? What does it mean to lead in love?

Our tests will not be "religious." Your "religion" rarely tells the true condition of your soul. The Bible says true religion is to "take care of orphans and widows in their sufferings and to keep yourself unspotted by the world."[7] Since both orphans and widows have been left leaderless, and since "unspotted by the world" means you submit not to your peer group but to God, authority and submission stand as keys to our inmost selves. "Religious" conversation always undershoots the target. Christ calls us to something more basic: a complete reorientation of personality. Abraham Maslow explains why: "People with low self-esteem tend to be more religious than people with high self-esteem. . . . A person who goes to church regularly may actually be rated as less religious than one who does not go to church at all because, perhaps (1) he goes to avoid social isolation, or (2) he goes to please his mother, or (3) religion represents for him not humbleness but a weapon of domination over others, or (4) it marks him as a member of a superior group, or (5) as in Clarence Day's father, 'It is good for the ignorant masses and I must play along.' Going to church can mean practically anything, and therefore, for us, practically nothing."[8] You cannot divide life into sacred and secular: religion and spirituality over here, business and family over there. It makes you cross-eyed. You look two ways at one time; you have no central focus: both eyes short out. But if your vision is single, "your whole body is full of light."[9] Secular Christianity is the only kind there is. Religious Christianity (not calling for practical obedience) is a false gospel. Christianity is full time or it is nothing. The Christ we worship is a secular Christ. In Jesus, God came down to earth. So our leadership tests will be down to earth too.

Am I Willing to Face Conflict?

Christian leadership's first essential is your willingness to fight. One of my sons wants me to call this whole chapter "Do Christians Fight Back?" He grew up afflicted by my immaturity. Isolated Bible verses like "love your enemies" and "turn the other cheek" had left me confused. Hypnotized, staring at the Bible's southern half, you can miss its stormy north. *Is* the Sermon on the Mount suicidal? *Is* Christianity defenselessness? *Is* fighting inherently wrong? Of course not. Scripture is never ridiculous. If my interpretation makes it ridiculous then my interpretation is wrong. Now I know better. Christ is the world's greatest fighter.

How did I get so mixed up? Long stories go better untold, but
one reason was my Baptist bent toward legalism. I figured the
Sermon on the Mount was a New Testament Ten Commandments. Law is lots easier than Grace. Finally I learned what the
Sermon on the Mount really is: *a description of happiness.*
Remember? It starts with the Beatitudes, the "blesseds," the
"happy are you's."[10] Rules can't bring you happiness, never,
never, never. Happiness comes out of relationships. And that's
what the Sermon—as well as the whole Bible—is about . . .
relationships. The Sermon on the Mount describes a mature relationship between God above and people below: a loving trusting
confident authority-submission relationship. Describing it—the
Sermon on the Mount set the tone for the rest of Jesus' life—
demonstrating it. "Turn the other cheek" is part of the picture but
only part. Turning the other cheek is submission. The rest of the
picture is authority. The sentence which finishes the Sermon on
the Mount says, "He taught them, not as the scribes, but as one
having authority."[11]

In Christ you lose your life—not to lose it, but—to find it.[12]
If your self-denial is Christian it will produce your self-assertion.
No Christian self-denial is ever suicidal. You love your neighbor
AS you love yourself. If you do not love yourself you cannot love
your neighbor. Self-hate is self-murder: you cannot love your
neighbor MORE than you love yourself. If you hate yourself
you're killing your potential to love: you're not "all there" to love
anybody else. Your maturity is only your self-love given away. All
love begins with self-love. The love of God is, first of all, love for
himself. God's love for us reaches out because he loves himself
solidly, securely, unshakably. The Velvet-Covered Brick is Crucified Self-Love. The cross is Jesus turning the other cheek. The
resurrection is Jesus fighting back. Christ fights only to hold his
rightful place of leadership. And so will you.

California illustrates. During the People's Park Protest, Berkeley authorities tried to negotiate with the Street People who demanded a ninety-nine-year lease on the Do-It-Yourself Park just
east of Telegraph Avenue. Berkeley's city officials offered a five-
year lease to the students' chief negotiator. He erupted: "If we
took that offer to the people they'd tear us apart." Berkeley City

Manager Hanley said, "It was like something out of *Lord of the Flies*. The leaders were frightened of their followers." Right. But you know what? I sympathize with that young student leader. I know about fearing your followers too. You don't need violence in the streets to be afraid of people under you. I've been scared up in front of audiences when I was speaking, by employees beneath me at work, and by my own kids at home. Berkeley is nothing special. There's no shortage any place: rebellious followers give you leaders getting scared.

Except in Christ. You can be unafraid—on top. "Perfect love casts out fear."[13] My own story is no Berkeley, but it gives me hope. Recently a big conflict exploded between me and one of my sons. About money. He was being financially irresponsible. I made him face facts. Discipline hurts. His fury grew, his eyes flashed fire. Finally he boiled over.

"Dad, how do you know what is right all the time? You're not God!"

I said to him laughing: "In this family I am."

To my family . . . I'm God? Don't laugh. Christ shared with all of us his value. So I am a residential representative of his function. I am a man, only a man and nothing but a man—to think otherwise is blasphemy—but in Christ I am a man fully. And full manhood means dominion. In the very first chapter of Genesis: "Be fruitful; multiply; fill the earth and subdue it; bear rule. . . ."[14] You were built for command. Within your limited boundaries you are the king. God has given his crown—cut down to your exact human size—to you.

For those under you that crown means discipline.

Reality therapist William Glasser and the impact of Transactional Analysis in contemporary psychiatry show you therapists using their authority, demanding that we use our authority too. "People who are not at sometime in their lives, preferably early, exposed intimately to others who care enough about them both to love and discipline them will not learn to be responsible. For that failure they suffer all their lives."[15] Glasser tells about his California Youth Authority work with delinquent girls. In one of his therapy groups was a girl named Liz. Each Monday her mother came to visit. Glasser suggested they include Liz's mother in the therapy group. The results were excellent. With the support of the group, Liz's mother changed from a seemingly helpless, manipulated, guilt-ridden, inadequate woman to someone who now began to play the mother's role with some authority. "In the beginning her mother whined that Liz would only run away again as she had done in the past when she insisted on proper behavior, but the group hammered home to the mother that it was her job to call the parole officer when Liz broke rules. She was told that it would show she did not really love Liz if she did not do so. The group demanded discipline and Liz began to demand it too. She agreed that perhaps she could be different if her mother would call her bluff."[16] The absence of discipline is the absence of love. "Do your child the favor of telling him how you feel," says Haim Ginott. "Parents willing to suffer the pain of their child's intense anger," says Glasser, convince him "I care enough about you to force you to act in a better way."[17]

Jesus of Nazareth or Pontius Pilate? Whose leadership style do I choose? In organizational dialogue Jesus said to Pilate, "You have authority over me only because it was given you by God."[18] To every one of us—governors, supervisors, foremen, teachers, adults —he says the same: "You have authority because it was given you by God." Leadership: not privilege but responsibility. Glasser said, "Parents willing to suffer. . . ." Love unafraid to lead; love willing to fight back. But not Pilate. He chose no conflict, no suffering, no fight: no leadership. Pilate's style was leadership's forfeit: the spectacle of a leader afraid. Forsaking authority, playing the politics game, letting the mob have his job—he washed his hands.

In my house I don't claim to be perfect, but I do claim to be in charge. You either make up your mind to "exert yourself to lead" or else—you wind up with scared hands in the water basin.

Do I Make People Comfortable?

Is leadership conflict or comfort?
Both.
Spontaneous, flexible, moral originality: you make conflict com-

fortable. Two words come to us out of the Bible about how Authority functions. Both are essential.

"Justification."

"Sanctification."

(1) "Justification" is the word for *acceptance*. I accept you as you are because God accepts me as I am. "Justification by faith" means you accept the gift of your acceptance. I do not have to reform, do better, improve, figure it out, straighten up, fly right, fulfill the law—or anything else—before I come to Christ. I come just as I am. In spiritual poverty, bankrupt before God, I take my acceptance as a beggar takes a free gift. All I need is to know my need. On the security of Christ's cross—a sacrifice for me complete, finished, perfected—I am totally, absolutely completely accepted. "Justification": just as if I'd never sinned. Golgotha's agony enables a Holy God to accept a sinful man like me and still be Holy himself. The Judge—the righteous Father—in the person of his Son—himself takes the rap. Your faith accepts the gift. "Being justified by faith we have peace with God."[19] Then justification becomes contagious. "Just as I am" I've been accepted; now I can accept you *just as you are*. Peace with God and peace with each other come in a package: God makes me comfortable so I can make you comfortable.

(2) "Sanctification" is the word for *change*. Contagious justification is not enough. We also need contagious sanctification.

Justification: God accepts me as I am.

Sanctification: God accepts me as I can be.

"Sanctification" means *set apart, holy, saintly, distinct, different:* it speaks of process. Justification: the completed relationship, Sanctification: the growing fellowship. . . . Justification: the pleasure, Sanctification: the pain. . . . Justification: Jesus loves me, this I know, Sanctification: I get to know who he is. . . . Sanctification looks hopeless to anybody but God: he is turning me into a saint. He takes me just as I am but he will not leave me that way; I'm in for complete overhaul. Habitual conversion. A caterpillar becomes a butterfly—but it hurts.

Why does it hurt? Because—Jesus below, reflecting God above —the highest order in any species reflects the nature of the species above it. Monkeys are not unusual acting like monkeys. But we put them on television when they act like men. Lassie is famous because she reflects human personality—a dog above dogs. How did Lassie get that way? A man (the species above) entered into constructive conflict with her (we call it animal training) and got his thinking into her mind. So Lassie became the world's most honored dog. She may not appreciate it, but her pain constitutes her highest compliment. Her leader trains her by mutual suffering.

Creative suffering like Lassie's goes in two directions—both up and down. Lassie suffers (down), but think (up) about her trainer! Patience is his diet each morning for breakfast. If I had the time I'd be more patient myself. I can take anything—except suffering. I make little jokes here because the truth gets too close. The heart of Authority is suffering. Beyond my comprehension: "The Lamb slain from the foundations of the world." "Love suffers long":[20] Patience is love stretched out. You look at Authority and all you can see is a cross: Suffering up and down. "It was clearly fitting that God should, in bringing many sons to glory, make the leader who delivers them perfect [mature] through sufferings."[21] God suffering—down. "God was in Christ, reconciling the world to himself, not counting their trespasses against them."[22] God suffering—up. In Christ suffering has two directions: up to the leader; down to the led.

Conflict made comfortable: My suffering is not the issue; the issue is my obedience. My suffering is inevitable, but victory over it demands my will. Authority springs from obedience, relies on obedience, is obedience, incarnate. Your freedom to rule lies hidden—in your loyalty to obey. Why? Because God obeys; he obeys himself: he cannot violate his character, his nature, his love. In Hosea, God—the brokenhearted, the lover betrayed—cries, "How can I give you up, O Ephraim? How can I hand you over, O Israel? My heart recoils. . . . My compassion grows. . . . I will not . . . I will not . . . for I am God and not man, the Holy One in your midst."[23] The Sovereign of the universe groans in agony, obedient to his inmost being. You worship a God who IS suffering-obedient-love: the cross is God's obedience. "The God of all comfort."[24]

Leadership is not something you *do;* it is something you *are.*
Jesus said, "You shall be witnesses to me."[25] Why didn't he say,
"You shall *do* witnessing"? Because so easily we fall in that trap:
doing but not being. George Macdonald warns us: "To try too
hard to make people good is to make them worse. The only way
to make them good is to be good, remembering well the beam and
the mote. The time for speaking comes rarely, the time for being
never departs."[26] In Levy's Delicatessen where I eat is a Viveka-
nanda quotation: "The moment you think you are 'helping,' you
undo the whole thing."

Comfortable relationships with an inherent integrity—these
relationships accept conflict, thrive on it, grow in every fight.
Remember Paul's relationship with the church in Corinth? It was
a long, drawn-out storm, a big roaring tempest—over his authority. Yet to that particular church in that immediate conflict he
wrote: "For as we share abundantly in Christ's sufferings, so
through Christ we share abundantly in comfort too. If we are
afflicted it is for your comfort . . . as you share in our sufferings
you will also share in our comfort."[27]

You have got to experience this paradox for yourself. Describing
it is tough. Christian leadership is mostly unconscious. Paul fought
—a tiger for his authority in Corinth. History found him convinc-
ing; still he touches the world. Why? Because Paul loved—an
unselfconscious love for those he led. Committing your will to
Christ is both continuous and conscious. But his Spirit forms the
life of Christ in your unconscious. What does it mean to be
Christlike? I don't know fully yet. But not self-conscious piosity.
When I stumble on this point I usually find I'm straining for
religious dominance; bossing but not serving. Presumption claims
leadership it doesn't have. Faith exercises leadership naturally.
Christ in you is normal and natural and relaxed. Any man filled
with the Holy Spirit will impress you preeminently with his quiet
calm sanity.[28] Full of Christ, you become *aware.* You sense what
people around you want and need so they can be at ease. You make
them comfortable without thinking about it. In Christ's story on
the last judgment, those who gave cups of water in his name, who
clothed the naked and fed the hungry, who visited the sick and

imprisoned—who found they had served the incognito Christ (the least of these my brethren)—*didn't even remember what they had done!*[29] Second-nature love: not what they did; what they were. They made people comfortable, unconsciously.

"Do-it-this-way" rules and techniques only make it harder. Your human relationships flow from your one big relationship with God: get all your thinking concentrated. Jesus called the Holy Spirit another "Comforter" . . . another like himself.[30] "Comforter" in the Greek original meant *advocate.*[31] Advocate? Yes, an advocate is someone who pleads your cause, someone who is on your side, someone who is for you . . . regardless. The Holy Spirit is your enthusiast, your encourager, your promoter. In me, he is that same thing for you. To be fully human you need significance; you have to feel important. Rationally, Christ's death tells you how great you are. Emotionally, others get it across to you. You begin to recognize your real value. You feel like somebody big, someone a smart talent scout would die for.

Driving in the car that day, how did we happen to be talking about funerals? Stephen had just been to his first funeral; I guess that was the background. And I had been asked to give a eulogy at a friend's memorial service. Stephen, Debbie, and I were traveling along Santa Fe Street north toward home in the car. Debbie wanted more information.

"What happens at funerals?"

"Well, uh . . ." I was getting ready to answer when Stephen spoke first.

"You play up their good points," he said.

A theology of eulogies. The good point for any of us is that Christ died and rose again. So now we live in an atmosphere not of death but resurrection, not of condemnation but affirmation. Not for funerals but for everyday: eulogies for the living. In your presence, to your face, I eulogize you: the resurrection relationship style—I affirm you. Dead relationships come alive. "Count yourselves dead to sin but alive to righteousness."[32] *Yourselves:* plural. Count your fellow man dead to his sins but alive to his righteousness. "Love believes all things."[33] Wisely, appropriately, I look for the good in you to affirm. "Neither do I condemn you: go and sin no more. . . . Be whole of your plague. . . . Rise, take up your bed and walk."[34] You can walk, you can do it, you can be a new person, I believe God is working in you. "There is therefore now no condemnation for those who are in Christ Jesus."[35] Do you condemn those around you or do you affirm them? Everyday eulogies. The God of all comfort, the God of affirmation, the God who gives you a boost. Not flattery. Not manipulation. Not soft soap. I play up your good points. Your low self-esteem gets built up high. Your good points include your potential: the real and possible you. I build you up: the power of suggestion. Coaching by affirmation and the genius of Harry Hopman built an Australian dynasty in world tennis. He had a slow-footed boy; he nicknamed him "Rocket"; he had a weak, frail one so he named him "Muscles"; Rocket Rod Laver and Ken Muscles Rosewall, champions by affirmation. Remember the disciple who was impetuous, mercurial and rash? Peer pressure molded him like putty. What did Jesus name him? Just the opposite: *Petros*, Peter; the Rock. Not what he was but what he could become: transformed in affirmation. Creative conflict. Love makes the real you comfortable.

Do I Make the Other Person Great?[36]

You find Laity Lodge in the country of 1,100 springs—"Frio" means *Cold* River—hidden in the vastness of the Texas Edwards Plateau mountains. Up high, looking down on the fish, the boats, and the swimmers below, its great hall juts out—cantilevered above the lake. For twelve years this place, dedicated to God, has spoken as an innovative center about renewal—for persons, families, and churches; for clergy and laymen of all kinds, sorts, sizes and descriptions; for all denominations. In addition to my grocery-company load, its work got very heavy, so Keith Miller, an Episcopal oilman friend, came to help. Keith had then just finished an Earlham College graduate degree in religion under Elton Trueblood.

Keith Miller was superb at Laity Lodge. He and I had great fun as our teams and formats developed. I left business behind on the weekends and traveled up for the retreats. Groups from all over

Texas were coming, a kind of ecumenicity at the grass roots. Keith and I shared the speaking load. Small groups, panel discussions, and counseling took up our schedules. After each conference I packed my family up to fly or drive back for our H.E.B. merchandising meeting on Monday morning. Time kept charging by; my company pressures grew heavier. By then Laity Lodge was humming. So as others came to help Keith I went less frequently myself, staying in touch by phone. And one day—during one of those telephone conversations—Keith told me he was working on a book.

It was no surprise; I had encouraged him to write. But way down deep the news jolted me: I wanted to write myself. Now here I was, grubbing it out in the grocery business, covered over by prunes and pinto beans and pepper sauce, making the money so Keith Miller could sit up there in the hills and write *his* book! Black ink on grocery ads kept reminding me of Miller by that blue-green lake. Revising a two-page spread, I'd think of Miller lounging in a deck chair; me sweating out double-truck deadlines, him retreating cool and quiet to write. The more I sweated the madder I got. I worked myself up into a first-class Christian snit.

My wife first confronted me at home.

"Howard, Keith's book is bothering you."

"Who, me?"

Then Bill Cody, organizing our Layman's Leadership Institutes, came to Corpus Christi. He touched the same nerve.

"Howard, Keith threatens you in a way I don't. Why don't you accept your place? Your greatness is to make Keith great."

We sat in my car outside the grocery company office when that comment from Bill Cody slugged me. I felt it in the pit of my stomach. I left him and went to my office. I closed the door. I prayed.

"Lord Jesus, I commit to you my feelings about Keith and his book. I'm helpless to handle this on my own. Thank you for handling it in your death and resurrection. Amen."

Within a few days I admitted to Keith my sin of jealousy. We had a good laugh; the stress was gone. *The Taste of New Wine* became a modern phenomenon in religious publishing. For me the best part of the story was my own elation about Keith's success. When I told him about Cody's saying, "Your greatness is to make Keith great," Keith answered: "Howard, leadership like that is a gift of grace."

My lesson was invaluable. Golembiewski says we operate by Christian principles when "supervisors at all levels rely less on what might be called 'inhibiting authority' whose purpose it is to keep people from going wrong—rather, the emphasis is upon 'helping authority,' that is, providing the resources that permit people to grow and produce."[37] Christ's grace in me makes Christian principles come alive. Without his grace I'm sunk. Carl Rogers calls it to be a facilitator.[38] Kenotic leadership. *Kenosis* means self-emptying. The serving son, the ruling father's equal: pouring a square glass of water into a round glass, you still have all the water. Serving can never demean you; humility is heaven's throne. The kenotic Christ makes you into a facilitator. Authority helping.

Management teaches us about the power-pie. How much power does my department have in the company? How much power do I have in my own department? Imagine for a moment I am your boss; you are a member of my team. If I keep control of every decision the power-pie is all mine. If I decentralize our decision-making then I share the power-pie with you. When the power-pie is cut up more ways, the boss's share does not get smaller: it gets larger. The whole pie grows. "If a manager permits his subordinates to exercise influence on what goes on in his department, does he have correspondingly less influence?" The research of management sociologist Rensis Likert says No . . . a powerful argument for submission on the part of bosses. "The manager's leadership methods, including the extent to which he builds his men into a well-knit loyal group, affect the amount of authority the manager really has. Giving the men more influence gives the managers more influence. They have actually increased the size of the influence-pie. . . ."[39] Do you think Keith Miller's book has hurt or helped Laity Lodge? His greatness makes me greater too.

Friendship: the new style for leaders, the new atmosphere for organizations. "No longer do I call you servants, but I have called you friends. . . . Greater love has no man than this, that a man lay down his life for his friends."[40]

Can I Be Vulnerable and Open?

If your leadership is Christian you can openly reveal your failures. Leaders who are fully human do not hide their sins. Within you operates the principle of the cross, the modus operandi of *strength in weakness*.

This principle points up our problem—we who are religious. We want a Christian reputation more than we want Christ. And yet our Lord, becoming sin for us, "made himself of no reputation."[41] Unlike him we flaunt our successes and hide our failures. Not Christ. The cross was loud. Mobs, shouting, screaming, rumbling, thundering, lightning, earthquake: "with a loud cry Jesus died."[42] The cross was loud but the resurrection was quiet. A silent gray dawn broken by the scraping of a stone and then . . . Sunrise. The cross is a human God revealing his defeat; resurrection shows you that divine failure triumphant. He told us little about his resurrection body; he appeared to believers only; resurrection is understatement. But his cross leaves us limp, crushed in narrative detail. Strange biographies, these Gospels: they focus mostly on the Hero's death, his failure, his weakness— the open unashamed cross. The story teaches you *Hidden Power served by Weakness Revealed.*

Am I willing to hide my strengths and reveal my weaknesses? Are you? Telling our triumphs, our successes, our achievements, we glorify ourselves. The central issue of life is the glory of God. "What is the chief end of man?" asks the catechism. "Man's chief end," we learn, "is to glorify God and enjoy him forever."[43] Paul said, "We preach not ourselves."[44] Do I preach myself or Jesus Christ? Am I my own righteousness or is Christ my righteousness? Your freedom in admitting your sins is the gauge for God's glory in you. Saints have the most sins; they are the freest to admit them. It doesn't mean they monopolize the market. "He who conceals his transgressions will not prosper, but he who confesses and forsakes them will obtain mercy."[45] Bragging about my good-

ness, I build barriers up; when I confess my sins, those barriers
come down. Pagan outsiders get driven away by our pious parade
of religious achievements. Building our high walls of intimidation,
we make their friendly corner bartender look good. Christians are
not half-angels with high-beam halos, but real live forgiven sinners
up close.

Sometimes the Bible strikes new readers as sordid and seamy.
But why should it shock you? In the Bible God revealed his
people's weaknesses. That is its power. The Bible honors God
realistically; the wrath of man praises him.[46] I love Simon Peter
because I crave popularity too; I love James and John because I
am ambitious, as they were; I love David because I fight battles
with lust like him: these men help me find victory by being open
about their defeats. The principle of the cross—the principle of
openness—is the principle of the Scripture.

"In the cross of Christ I glory."[47] Establishing the fact of his
leadership, Jesus didn't brag. His character confirmed his words
unspoken. Did he ever say "I love you" to any individual among
his followers? If so we don't know it. Why not? Why didn't he
trumpet his own goodness? Because the cross spoke the language
of our weakness, the spilled eloquence of blood, the word in flesh
crucified. John wrote "God is love" by what he saw Jesus to be.[48]
Love never reveals itself by strutting. You point to God's righteousness and not to your own. To yourself you die.

"Confess your sins to one another and pray for one another that
you may be healed," says St. James's Epistle.[49] Confession gives
you mutual acceptance—an atmosphere of shared humanity.
Prayer's intelligent love completes the climate. Conflict finishes
off James's passage on Christian health: "whoever brings back a
sinner from the error of his way. . . ."[50] Your conflicts layered in
with your confessions turn healthy. For a therapeutic atmosphere
you mix eulogies, conflict, confession, and prayer together. "Awakening in the church will not come," says Karl Olsson, "until we
come to grips with emotional healing."[51] Confession kicks off the
cycle of compassion. Both starting the Christian life and also
continuing it, you pray, "Oh Lord, I am a sinner . . . I confess my
sins . . . I turn from my sins. . . ." Confession of sin starts you in

Christ and continues you too. You don't confess abstract, imaginary, unreal sins. You're after real, down-to-earth, solid, practical stuff. In my relationships redemption gets at my guts.

Isn't confession dangerous? Of course it is. Dangerous like dynamite. Don't play with it unawares: leadership demands discipline. Confession of sin can be sick. Openness can be a disease. Brutal confession is not love but domination and tyranny. Confession of sin can be my way to hurt you. I've got to face my motives.

Obedience is the key word about our openness. "If we confess our sins he is faithful and just to forgive us our sins and to cleanse us from all unrighteousness": the I John 1:9 recipe. Confession is first, foremost, and essentially to God. You confess the specific sin: you thank God for his finished forgiveness. It is complete between God and you alone; the essential transaction is closed. Then (second and separate transaction), if it lies in your own personal path of obedience, if it will be constructive—*only* if it will be constructive—you confess to others. Forgiveness comes to you on the sole exclusive basis of Christ's sacrificial blood; "not by works of righteousness which we have done."[52] We never confess in order to be forgiven; we confess because we are forgiven already. I confess my sins to others if it is helpful, appropriate, and wise. Christ within you is wisdom: lots of times he tells you to thank him and shut up.

Christ's death frees you from hiding your sins. You can be vulnerable and open. When you are weak then you are strong.[53] You shake the darkness with irresistible blows: the divine might of weakness. You hit your hardest when your guard is down.

Tonight I relive our family drama these past few weeks at Corpus Christi's Ray High School. Young Howard is an upcoming senior, campaigning for next year's Student Council presidency. His slogans are political jewels:

"Butt Power"
"Howard Butt: He's the Living End"
"Get the Council off its Rear: Vote Butt"

High inspiration and low humor you cannot fight. Several weeks ago things looked good for Howard: it was in the bag. Then, catastrophe. Following the crucial speeches to the student assembly and the casting of the votes, Butt was disqualified! His speech, along with his nominators', was one minute forty-five seconds overtime. This infraction, along with other technical controversies, moved the outgoing Student Council to disqualify him without counting the ballots. His opponent would get it by default.

Gloom, doom, sadness, and grief.

But wait.

Stirrings behind the scenes.

The opponent didn't want it that way. Howard was called in by the outgoing council. He went. They talked. They changed their decision. The votes were counted. And . . . *our man won!*

Oh fateful discussions.

Oh wise men, you students.

Oh fine young new leader:

"Howard, what did you say in that crucial council meeting?"

"Well, Dad, I just admitted my mistakes. That made them feel it was okay to change their minds. Then I asked them to count the votes and let the winner win."

"Blessed are the poor in spirit, for they shall inherit the Kingdom of God."[54]

Am I Fun to Live and Work With?[55]

Our first test about Christian authority was on conflict. This last one is on fun. It figures: "Joy to the world" comes when Love gets into the fight—Bethlehem was Round One. Our own fear of conflict incarnates our failure to love. Why do we miss having fun? I'll tell you why. Phony relationships. Unreal relationships give you the emotional fallout of boredom.

"It's not worth the hassle." How often did I use that excuse? Then I got convicted: my unwillingness to hassle showed up my lack of love. I didn't care enough to take the trouble or the time. Hassle is crucial in loving your kids. No substitute for hassle with your employees. "The highly effective group," says Likert, "does not hesitate to look at and deal with friction between its members.

By openly putting such problems on the table and sincerely examining them they can be dealt with constructively."[56] In *The Will to Manage* the distinguished McKinsey & Company business analyst Marvin Bower says, "The most outstanding chief executives seek out major problems. Weak chief executives, on the other hand, tend to avoid difficult problems and hope they will go away."[57] Christ in you is executive excellence. You care enough to hassle.

If you run from hassles you shut out joy: when you are willing to love you are unafraid to fight. Your relationships—now getting their own integrity—begin to deepen. Leadership *is* relationship. God is relationship: the relationship of Love. In every organization both the leader and the led are looking for love. Conflict is the rub between immature leaders in authority and immature followers in submission. God is perfect Authority and perfect Submission, both. In him there is no conflict. But we—imperfect people in an imperfect world—we have not got there yet. Therefore, we need this conflict; we should expect it—for our progress in God it is essential. Our sanctification rolls forward on the wheels of our conflicts. "All have sinned";[58] nobody perfect but God: your conflict is universal, inescapable, and pregnant with joy.

When my tension with Dad and Charles in our company was at its height, I was tempted to run. I wrote a letter of resignation. I was ready to move—Europe, New York, somewhere, anywhere —you name it. The letter was finished, ready to be delivered. Providentially that night my friend Bob Peerman of Peerman Homes dropped by our house for a visit. I showed him the letter. His face clouded. He turned on me like a prophet.

"If you start running, Howard, you'd better run a long way. And even then you'll face the same problems—with different people— somewhere else. I think it's a lousy letter. You're trying to escape."

I knew he spoke the truth. Charles and Dad loved me enough to hassle. I remembered a verse from the Bible: "In the world *you shall have tribulation,* but be of good cheer, I have overcome the world."[59] Don't run away from conflict, Howard. Cheer up in the middle of it.

Forgiveness is fun spreading out: Jesus brings you contagious reconciliation. "Forgive us our trespasses as we forgive those who trespass against us."[60] If you don't forgive you won't be forgiven. Did Jesus practice what he preached? No, he preached what he practiced, which is a lot harder to do. Being precedes doing: forgiveness started in the heart of God. Initiative from the top. "Of him are you in Christ Jesus."[61] God came down; God took the initiative. Forgiveness takes shoe leather. Like those Bible Society trustees who couldn't decide what material to use to bind a new issue of Bibles they'd printed. What kind of covers? Paper? Cloth? Or Persian Morocco? One trustee rose. "Mr. Chairman, I move we bind these Bibles in shoe leather and walk out their teachings in everyday life!" Bibles bound in shoe leather take forgiveness all over town. When Peter asked Jesus if forgiving his brother seven times was enough and Jesus answered, "No, seventy times seven," did he mean we should keep records?[62] Of course not; that's the point. Forgiveness becomes a habit. You forget to number instances because forgiveness is your regular systematic pattern. Forgiveness fills any group from the top. God above you teaches you how to forgive as a leader—without fouling up your leadership. Whipped-cream forgiveness is out. For you as a leader, forgiveness follows conflict in the open. The absence of construc- tive conflict—clearly recognized, creatively resolved—is the ab- sence of authentic love. Forgiveness is the framework whenever your conflicts get constructive. Every human relationship that stays healthy involves tension. Relationships without stress are either nonexistent, shallow, or sick. "If your brother commits a sin against you, go and take the matter up with him. . . ."[63] Your conflicts don't dry up unattended, they fester. Violence in a so- ciety is the accumulation of little conflicts ignored. If you keep current with God you keep current with people. "If when you are bringing your gift to the altar, you suddenly remember that your brother has a grievance against you, leave your gift where it is before the altar. First go and make peace with your brother, and only then come back and offer your gift. . . ."[64] Conflict with your brother takes precedence over religious routine. First go to your brother. Religion waits while you go. Pollution among people spews out from grievances soured: friendship needs fresh air. "Be angry and sin not."[65] How do you really feel? Keep short accounts. "Let not the sun go down on your wrath."[66] Make each day a package of peace. Love assumes the initiative. Eyeball to eyeball. Shoe-leather forgiveness. Jesus the Word calls us to communication.

Conflict and hassle is one route to family enjoyment; the other is our mutual interest in each other. I was slow to discover both these secrets of joy. "Look to each other's interests and not merely to your own."[67] When you get interested in what interests others, to those others you are truly fun. Joy is deeper than humor: it springs up wherever you go—if other people are your focus. The conversationalists I have met who really struck me as great got interested in what I was saying. If the attention you pay me is perceptive and affirming I guarantee to find you fascinating. "Perceptive" means you *see* me as I am. Joy is light: we *do* perceive each other; gloom is dark: you miss seeing the real me. Loving Authority takes an interest in whatever interests you.

Stephen was about nine when he got into Cub Scouts. My wife had just confronted me—eyeball on—about my time with him. She said in my schedule he was neglected. Howard's tennis took lots of my interest, but Stephen was getting ignored. Late one night at the kitchen table, Barbara Dan and I prayed about my time with Stephen.

Then came the Cub Scout's Pinewood Derby.

Do you ever hate the way God answers your prayers?

"Dad, when can we do this work on my Pinewood Derby racer?" Stephen stood in the kitchen doorway after supper, a clear plastic bag in his hand. Inside the bag I could see a block of soft-pine wood, ready for carving, along with some wheels and other accessories for a little racing car.

"It's a father-and-son project," he said.

I'm standing there breathing . . . stewing . . . dying inside.

Me a handicrafter? No thanks. Not me. I'm hopeless with my hands. Twelve thumbs. Surely I've got some other engagement. Doesn't somebody want me to preach? Go to a meeting? Do something religious? Careful, pal. There are lots of other preachers; Stephen has only one Dad. Namely, you. In charge of racing cars. You may be a second-class mechanic but you're called to be a first-class Dad. I had been torpedoed: there was no way out. I tossed up a silent prayer.

"Help!"

I dumped the bag out on the kitchen cabinet and started to commence to begin. You civilians may not know that the Cub Scouts provide very soft wood—prenotched for each of the four wheels and also for the driver's seat. They should. My wife has awful woodworking equipment in our kitchen. Soon I was sitting on the stool surrounded by her knives, my shavings, and a grim little cloud of resignation. But an uncanny thing began to happen . . . the racer started to look good! I got excited. The shavings were all over the kitchen floor, but in my hand by now there was emerging a miniature Maserati! I felt like Michelangelo in Detroit. An hour went by, then two. "More sandpaper." I needed more sandpaper. "Stephen, do we have any more . . . Stephen? Stephen! Where is Stephen? I thought this was a father-and-son project! Where is Stephen?"

"Oh, he's in the study watching television."

Finally I had it nearly done. Stephen wandered in, nonchalant. Then he saw the car. As I write this now I remember the surprise in his voice that night long years ago. He was shocked, amazed, thunderstruck. Daddies can come up with surprises that out-surprise all the other surprises of life. Our children know us so well. Any son knows when—in his own kitchen—he has seen a miracle. Stephen was stunned.

"Hey Dad, that looks great!"

Later that evening I went into the boys' room to say good night. Stephen lay in his bed, wide-eyed, staring at the ceiling.

"Buddy, why aren't you asleep?" I said.

"Dad," he said, "I've got the Pinewood Derby Fever."

Barbara Dan told me afterward that she overheard their talk as the two boys fell asleep.

Stephen: "Dad said he couldn't do that racer. My foot. He did it great!"

Howard: "Yeah, I know. He can do about anything if he puts his mind to it."

I started considering the Pinewood Derby business full time. Christ in me is fun for others. Not my interests, *his* interests; not my interests, *their* interests; not my interests, *interests outside myself.* If I'd only pray more I'd be more fun.

Let's summarize. The authority of love fights for itself creatively, accepting others as equals. It affirms them, helping them grow. Since loving authority is vulnerable and open, fighting creatively for itself turns out to be suffering in behalf of others. But, by love's mysterious alchemy, the whole process turns into unadulterated delight. I see myself as a leader. I'm really somebody . . . important, unique, special. I failed to see Keith's greatness making me great; I failed to see Stephen's fun making fun for me. I saw myself—not too big—but too small.

What a thought. Me . . . a king.

Sir, that is good news.

My own pastoral authority!

> If the day ever comes when they know who
> They are, they may know better where they are.
> But who they are is too much to believe—
> Either for them or for the onlooking world.[68]

IV

Submission: Key to Power

Count others better than yourselves.
Philippians 2:4

The crown of your Christian leadership is a crown of shining thorns. The crown of revolution disintegrates. The crown of submission is exalted. "Wherefore God has highly exalted him and given him a name above every name."[1] The pattern is eternal: you can see it everywhere. Two men marching up to you now illustrate it. You know their names: Saul and David. Saul pictures rebellion; David shows you submission. Two kings; two crowns; two styles: one exalted and one extinct. You find King Saul discarded and forgotten in history's dustbin. But—three thousand years later, still making headlines—you call Jerusalem the city of David, the city of the King.

King Saul got his instructions; he chose not to obey: the rebellion of royalty. You read the sad story in I Samuel: (1) It tells you why Saul rebelled against God's commands: his fear of his followers. "I feared the people and obeyed their voice."[2] Either you fear God or else you fear those under you. (2) It tells you why Saul's followers scared him: his low view of himself. "Though you are little in your own eyes, are you not the head? . . . The Lord appointed you king."[3] Your relation to God transforms your inner self-image. (3) It tells you how Saul's low self-image made him act: just the precise opposite. "He had gone to erect a monument to himself."[4] Feeling little, he acted big: God's glory or your own? (4) It shows you the root of Saul's leadership collapse: his proud stubborn unbelief. "You rejected the word of the Lord and the Lord rejected you from being king."[5] Rebellion carries the contaminated fallout of unbelief. (5) It shows you how rebellion justifies itself: by its own sacrifices. "Has the Lord as much pleasure in your sacrifice as in your obedience?"[6] You make sacrifices to avoid submission. (6) It tells you where rebellion will end: finally in suicide. "Saul took his own sword and fell upon it."[7] Self-justification leaves you no other way out. (7) It teaches you authority and submission—in the heartbreak of reverse. "Obedience is far better than sacrifice. . . . For rebellion is as bad as the sin of witchcraft, and stubbornness is as bad as worshipping idols."[8] In Saul you see rebellion's tragedy.

David was different: in him you see, not rebellion, but submission. Remember David at Ziph? From Ziph God zeroes in on you. If anyone anywhere anytime could make a case for revolution it was David at Ziph. He was not king yet; Saul still held the throne: poor-old-sad-old-sick-old Saul. And this same King Saul—jealous, frightened, full of hate—was out now to get David killed. Ever since Goliath, David's popularity had driven Saul—quite literally —out of his mind: rebellious leadership in the grip of paranoia. To save his life David fled. But his exile was not enough. Nothing would satisfy Saul but David's death, nothing cool the fire within his brain but blood. With three thousand select troops—and the help of Ziphite betrayal—Saul had now tracked David down. In the wilderness of Ziph Saul's sickness caught up with David's sanity.

> David slipped over to Saul's camp one night to look around. King Saul and General Abner were sleeping inside a ring formed by the slumbering soldiers.
> "Any volunteers to go down there with me?" David asked.
> "I'll go with you," Abishai replied. So David and Abishai went to Saul's camp and found him asleep, with his spear in the ground beside his head.
> "God has put your enemy within your power this time for sure," Abishai whispered to David. "Let me go and put that spear through him. I'll pin him to the earth with it—I'll not need to strike a second time!"
> "No," David said. "Don't kill him, for who can remain innocent after attacking the Lord's chosen king? Surely God will strike him

down some day, or he will die in battle or of old age. But God forbid I should kill the man he has chosen to be king!"[9]

You remember the rest of the story. David took the spear from beside Saul's head and, silent, slipped away. He climbed the face of the mountain opposite Saul's camp and from a safe distance called out, first to General Abner. Then he spoke to Saul.

"Here is your spear, sir. Let one of your young men come over and get it. The Lord gives his own reward for doing good and being loyal, and I refused to kill you. Now may the Lord save my life."[10]

A spear and a question: "Who can remain innocent after attacking the Lord's chosen king?"

Revolution or Submission?

Submission is everywhere implicit in the Old Testament. In the New Testament it becomes explicit. First you see it in our Lord's strategy—the submission of the cross. Then in full-orbed panoply the underlying ethical concept of submission is spelled out. St. Paul's famous 13th chapter of Romans applies submission to the organizational spectrum. "Let every person be subject to the governing authorities. For there is no authority except from God, and those that exist have been instituted by God. Therefore he who resists the authorities resists what God has appointed."[11] Now David's loyalty at Ziph has been universalized: every leader is God's appointed king. Christ says for you to love—not only the downtrodden, but also those on top. Surrounded by Roman tyranny, facing a Roman jail, Paul tells Christians in Rome to affirm every leader's potential: "He is God's servant for your good. . . . he is the servant of God. . . . the authorities are ministers of God."[12] Ephesians 5:21–6:9 and Colossians 3:18–4:1 apply submission to marriage, home, and work. I Timothy 2:1–3:13 and 5:17–6:2 discuss authority and submission in the church family. Counseling his protégé, Titus, about how to exercise leadership Paul writes, "Declare these things, exhort and reprove with all authority. Let no one disregard you. Remind them to be submissive to rulers and authorities, to be obedient . . . to show perfect courtesy toward all men."[13] Hebrews 13:7 says, "Obey your leaders and submit to them for they are keeping watch over you." The *longest* New Testament exposition of Christian submission comes, though, not in the writings of Paul but in the First Epistle of Peter. "Be subject for the Lord's sake to every human institution. . . . Servants, be submissive. . . . Wives, be submissive. . . . You that are younger be subject to your elders. Clothe yourselves with humility toward one another."[14] No one can find St. Peter unrealistic about what submission means: threading his entire epistle you get his encircling theme: the Christian and his suffering. He is teaching us the glory of the cross—power through pain. "Humble yourselves therefore under the mighty hand of God, that in due time he may exalt you."[15] It is as if today St. Peter says, "I kid you not—submission hurts. But it holds the key to your power."

Of course this doctrine is controversial. Since when was Truth an exercise in public consensus? Some say submission is unhealthy masochism. Others call it self-punishing futility. Others attack it as hopelessly out of date. Never fear, it is not. Submission is the inescapable path to power that lasts. David's submission cost him long years of waiting; he got his kingdom only in patience. But that submission gave him timeless authority; the Davidic kingdom reminds you of Israel's greatest king. Submission explains his name: "David" means "beloved chieftain." Submitting doesn't whittle you down, it builds you up. Humility is God's lifestyle. The way up is the way down. If you live to yourself you die; if you die to yourself you live. Submissive authority lasts.

Our modern and widespread idealization of revolution as the path for human progress is a relatively recent phenomenon. Out of all history's millennia past, revolution intellectualized is still under 250 years old. Its roots go back to the ancients and a Greek rather than a Judeo-Christian understanding of democracy. And also revolutionary millenarianism offers you tangled traces. But the doctrine itself—Equality by means of Revolution—(argued conceptually) remains very new. As God counts time it will not last long.

The idea of progress through revolution rests in part on our naïve glorification of the American Revolution, misunderstandings about it, and our worship, not of God but of the nation. Superpatriotism infects both right and left; chauvinism contaminates us all. Glamorizing revolution—in the name of America—is idolotrous nationalism. American-history books are not the Bible. In one sense the great modern revolutions—American and French in the eighteenth century, Russian and Chinese in the twentieth—all came from France. They came from the pen of Jean-Jacques Rousseau.

In 1749 Rousseau was out for a walk to visit his friend Diderot in Vincennes outside Paris. He took the *Mercure de France* to read as he walked. A prize offered by the Academy of Dijon for an essay on public morals caught his eye. He was thirty-seven, needing to make his name. Should he compete? What would he say? He described his revelation:

> All at once I felt myself dazzled by a thousand sparkling lights. Crowds of vivid ideas thronged into my mind with a force and confusion that threw me into unspeakable agitation; I felt my head whirling in a giddiness like that of intoxication. A violent palpitation oppressed me. Unable to walk for difficulty in breathing, I sank down under one of the trees by the road, and passed half an hour there in such a condition of excitement that when I rose I saw that the front of my waistcoat was all wet with tears. . . . Ah, if ever I could have written a quarter of what I saw and felt under that tree, with what clarity I should have brought out all the contradictions of our social system! With what simplicity I should have demonstrated that *man is by nature good, and that only our institutions have made him bad.*[16]

Rousseau's downfall was his theology. Intellectual submission was the issue: Rousseau was a literary Saul. If "man is by nature good" Jesus did not need to die, Adam and Eve are heroes, the Bible is applesauce. If "man is by nature good" you accept Rousseau but you reject Scripture: "No one is good, no one in the whole world is innocent. No one has ever really followed God's paths, or even truly wanted to. Everyone has turned away; all have gone wrong. No one has kept on doing right; not one."[17] Man's institutions are bad because man is bad; man cannot be separated from his institutions: you cannot make a good omelet out of rotten eggs. Jesus said, "No one is good except God alone."[18] Only God makes good institutions.

Mysteriously dividing men from their institutions—good men, bad institutions—with our additional light from the personality sciences: today it seems preposterous. Even a glimpse of Rousseau's childhood explains his institutional disenchantment, his distrust of authority. His childhood was tragic. Afterward his emotional reactions left his intellect enslaved. His personal relationships as an adult formed a chain of catastrophes, each bound to his paranoia. His marriage to his long-time mistress, Thérèse Lavasseur, just before his death, completed a tragic cycle—each of their five children at birth had been deposited in a foundling asylum. Rousseau's persecution mania colored all his thought— force justly overthrows what force has set up and maintained: you justify revolution. It has a modern sound: from Rousseau to Hegel to Marx; from Rousseau to Nietzsche to Hitler. Rousseau would recoil from modern totalitarian misuse of his ideas, but his concept of General Will makes the one-party state supreme. He thought he argued for democracy, but his starting premise was wrong: revolution instead of submission. By 1789 France tasted revolutionary blood. "After October 6, 1789, the Jacobins controlled Paris and Rousseau was their god."[19] Edmund Burke said of the French Revolutionary Constituent Assembly (1789–1791): "There is a great dispute among their leaders which of them is the best resemblance of Rousseau. In truth, they all resemble him. . . . him they study, him they meditate. . . . Rousseau is their Canon of Holy Writ."[20] Rousseau, who died in 1778, had not intended violence and massacre. But "in the beginning was the word":[21] the bad seed of bad ideas sprouts bad fruit. Robespierre sent Hébert to the guillotine feeling he followed Rousseau to the letter.[22] Revolution on the bottom equals tyranny on the top: the Reign of Terror.

February 28, 1972 the governments of the United States and the People's Republic of China issued a joint communiqué at the close of President Nixon's trip to China. The government of

China said then, "People want revolution—this has become the irresistible trend of history." Rousseau thought that too, in 1749. The atheist Voltaire perceived immediately where Rousseau's thinking would lead. He rebuked him. "You paint in very true colors the horrors of human society. . . . no one has ever employed so much intellect to persuade men to be beasts." Revolutionary philosophy is fundamentally irrational. Negative. Destructive. Dead. Historians Will and Ariel Durant, in their book *Rousseau and Revolution,* said, "Emotionally Rousseau remained always a child. . . . [Thérèse] remained permanently adolescent mentally, he remained permanently adolescent morally. . . . with all his consciousness of genius he never achieved self-respect."[23] He never saw himself a servant-king. The Durants said, "Politically we are only now emerging from the age of Rousseau."[24] The communiqué from the government of China was mistaken. The irresistible trend of history is *not* revolution: the irresistible trend of history is submission. Rousseau rejected the word of the Lord, and the Lord rejected him from being king.

Authority from the Bottom Up

A man told me recently about his visit to a psychologist. He needed help, he said, about his tensions. He said he was kept back from his full capacities in his work by his anxieties. So he sought out psychological counseling. The psychologist gave him some verbal tests:

"Now a thought-completion test. I want you to finish an unfinished sentence. Complete this statement for me with the very first words that pop into your mind. Are you ready?"

"Ready."

"Fine. Complete after me—'If you love me you will . . . ?' "

"If you love me you will . . . *do what I want you to do!*"

This man—the patient—after his visit to the psychologist's office rehearsed his test for me. But before he told me his answer he let me complete the sentence-question for myself; I also took the test. Our response was identical; we finished the statement exactly alike. Then he told me the psychologist had criticized his answer! *Our* answer! It really shook me up. I'm considering becoming a patient myself. Rejection by a psychologist makes me very tense. But . . . I've decided not to go. I got to imagining that poor psychologist if he had proposed the thought-completion sentence and my friend had refused—flat-out refused—to take the test! Can't you see him . . . smiling a professional smile? One tester-psychologist getting tense! Testers function by love too. "If you love me you'll do what I want you to do." So now once again I'm relaxed. You submit when you do what I want you to do.

Love asks for submission. Tonight my wife and I sit discussing this principle at dinner. Debbie is at summer camp, away for a month. Barbara Dan enthuses about how much our daughter enjoys getting mail. So what is happening? My wife is promoting mail for Debbie—recruiting the whole family to write our littlest camper! Brothers, grandparents, aunts, uncles, daddies, all of us are enlisted to brighten Debbie's mail-call. What gives mothers such great power with their children? Precisely this quality: Barbara Dan is doing what Debbie wants her to do. Love submits; the mother serves: submission is power.

Our next topic—after Debbie's mail—for our dinnertable conversation is a problem we face with an employee. He has been asked repeatedly to perform a routine ordinary job in his line of duty. These requests he has consistently ignored. What to do now? At the simplest level he does not love the person who directs his work—so he rebels. He need not be bloodthirsty or dramatic to rebel—his revolt is more like everyday sandpaper. But one consequence is inevitable. His refusal to follow instructions does not give him power in the organization—just the opposite—his power is diminished. The organization as a whole is hurt; we are all weakened when he is powerless.

My wife has more power with me than anyone else on earth. She influences everything from the way I cut my hair to the shoes I wear on my feet. She influences my decisions, my time, my recreation, my habits, my work, my thinking, my actions. Who gave this particular brown-haired woman such authority with me, such power? God gave it to her through her submission. She does what I want her to do. I don't understand perfectly how this works but the results are inescapably obvious to us all. The more my wife submits to me the more influence with me she has—her power is in her submission.

The story with which this book began—from my own life—shows you the submission principle at work in business. Why does my brother run our companies today? He did what Dad wanted him to do: submission is power. Dad's decision to entrust the business to Charles was inevitable: authority flows from submission. My own power with both Dad and Charles comes from the same source—I am doing what they want me to do—submission is my power too.

"Leadership is a relationship between a person exerting influence and those who are influenced," says social scientist E. P. Hollander in his book *Leaders, Groups, and Influence.*[25] He conducted a broad study of Naval Aviation Cadets. He calls his analyses "sociometry." He found that "followership" is not so much passive as active. There is a high degree of relation between leadership and followership. The most desired followers tended to be chosen from the upper choices as leaders. "Followership," he concluded, "holds within itself an incipient state of leadership."[26] For me to learn to lead is for me to learn to follow. Love is power; love is organization: you organize organization by your submission. Rebellious organizations get powerless. Friendship is Christ's new organizational style. On top the leader becomes your friend. Underneath you are called to be a friend too. Followership is friendship's underside. "You are my friends if you do what I command you," said Jesus. "No longer do I call you servants but I have called you friends."[27] Friendship from the top down. Friendship from the bottom up.

Rebelling reflects your insecurity; submitting, you show your calm sure sense of strength. Saul and Rousseau revealed why. Saul was "little in his own eyes"; Rousseau "never achieved self-respect." Love's submissive authority wins because it doesn't fear losing. Rebellion's tyrannical slavery loses by fearing defeat. Rebellion is competitive struggle; submission is triumphant assurance. Rebellion is exhausted works; submission is grace-filled being. Rebellion is win-lose strife and warring; submission is peaceful obedi-

ence. Thinking of your life as obedience to God you forget your
fear of failure. Why am I afraid to lose? Self-esteem. Losing
threatens my self-esteem—my self-image can't stand it. But every
man is a loser. Death is the final defeat; at the last, unalterably you
lose. No one can escape it: "once to die."[28] Christ took our defeat
upon himself, turning it into our victory. Winning is Christ's kind
of life; he even wins losing: a cross becomes a resurrection. Triumph is who he is: submission doesn't scare you; you've become
immune to defeat. "I have been crucified with Christ, nevertheless I live, yet not I but Christ lives in me."[29] Christ in you makes
submission authoritative: you rationally esteem yourself; your inner integrity is inviolable. The more thoroughly you are submitted
to God the more rational becomes your basis for self-respect. You
no longer fear submission; obedience is the issue: you are not afraid
to lose.

Conventional wisdom has thought of power as flowing from the
top down. In all of our organizations we think about authority as
the man who's "got it in the bag" on top: authority is the big bag
on top. Jesus came to give us a better way to think. He came down.
He came down to show us something new, something we hadn't
thought of: authority from the bottom up. "There is some justification for regarding the follower," says F. H. Sanford, "as the
most crucial factor in any leadership event."[30] Of course there is:
submissiveness is love organized. Chester Barnard shows you why
he is so revered among students of management. He speaks the
new wisdom: a man's authority is determined by his subordinates.[31] The Judeo-Christian idea of democracy rests on leadership as *the consent of the governed*. Barnard says, "Authority is
another name for the willingness of individuals to submit."[32] The
Father could not be the Father without the Son. Leadership is a
gift from people under you. The Son could not be the Son without
the Father. Submission is God giving leadership to you. Paul
Torgersen's *A Concept of Organization* is Chester Barnard
popularized. "Most people think of authority as originating at the
top of an organization," he says. "It filters downward in lessening
amounts from the top until it reaches the bottom where none
remains."[33] But you can also see authority as acceptance from

underneath. It flows from the bottom up, originating in the willingness of the participants to serve the leader. This is the way of the new humanity, the way of the obedient son, the way of God in human flesh. The leader serves the organization; the organization serves the leader; the two become one. Good institutions are possible: in Christ brotherhood is functionally practical.

The Bible's picture for this new organizational style in the world is marriage. I hope soon to have out a book on authority-and-submission, sex, and the family. For now let me say only this. The most dramatic human portrayal of authority-and-submission's power is sex. The woman's submission under him makes the man a leader. Her submission is physical power: jointly they produce a child. The child gives its parents the golden gift: together they receive leadership's gift bestowed on them out of their baby's rich treasure of dependence. Children create leadership out of their humility below us. The man asserts; the woman submits: creativity is yielding. Have you heard of any male mothers? Submission is the only difference between love and rape.

Sex is specialization. The man does his part; the woman does her part: specialization creates new life—in sex and everywhere. "Organization and specialization are synonyms" says Barnard. "The ends of cooperation cannot be accomplished without specialization. . . . The work of cooperation is not a work of leadership, but of organization as a whole."[34] The great Continental theologian Emil Brunner says, "There is always a subordination alongside equal dignity. The one must be above, the other below, the one must lead, the other obey. Wherever men have to do something together, there must be a hierarchy of competence, of command; where this is not recognized, the cooperative unit falls to pieces."[35] Equality together with hierarchy: Christ makes possible human unity. Plato was right: "a government which is united, however small, cannot be moved."[36] Velvet-covered bricks together: the style under Christ of the Church in the world. All this is God's purpose in giving you your gifts. Specialization is the purpose of gifts. Christ's kind of organization is united specialization, explosive with new power. "To organize, specialize."

Defining the structure is crucial to our organizational health.

Leadership can't work undefined; every human group demands it: government, employment, education, athletics, home. Without pupils under her, who is a teacher? Without a team to direct, who is a coach? Without citizens beneath him, who is a governor? Acceptance of authority above us in any human organization is acceptance of the authority of God. Submission to a leader—in the fear of God—invigorates the leader, vitalizes the organization, and rejuvenates the follower. In their book *Power and Morality in a Business Society* Sylvia and Benjamin Selekman say, "In this day social and moral imperatives carry with them not the giving up of things but the giving up of absolute, unilateral power."[37] Structure is prerequisite to security: God as Holy Trinity means that God is structure; look at your organizations from the Boss's viewpoint. Structure is your skeleton; submission is your muscle. Structure without submission is dead bones; submission without structure is hamburger. Is the organizational chart clear? Who's in charge? Structure tells me what is expected; I am told how I'm doing. I get the discipline I need: to support what is right, to correct what is wrong. I'm informed ahead of time on changes that will affect me; the structure prepares me for the future.[38] When conflict comes, consult the structure—it will give you light. The structure tells you when to command and when to obey. Are you fighting the structure or accepting it? God changes structures through your submission. Goethe pricks us to prayer:

> When are men most useless, would you say?
> When they can't command and can't obey.[39]

In any smoothly functioning cooperative venture you are in, this command-and-obey process goes on—inescapable, continuous, and unconscious. The structure and the specialization mesh in the relaxed atmosphere of authoritative submission. Torgersen explains how it works so flexibly. A janitor enters the office of a university president after normal working hours to clean up. The president is still at his desk working on papers. As quietly and unobtrusively as possible, the janitor sweeps, dusts, and empties ashtrays. But after a time the janitor decides he must disturb the president to sweep under his desk. He coughs, gets the president's attention, and asks the president to slide his chair back. The president slides his chair back—at the janitor's direction—and the janitor finishes up his service! A university's complex structure may contain thousands of "unit organizations" like this, fleshing out the structure's skeleton. The purpose was sweeping under the university president's desk: a service important to the overall health and purpose of the school—pig-pen academia discourages your learning. The "unit organization" was formed and then unformed in a matter of moments: in reality it was *a cooperative spirit* between the two men. It would be hard to picture on any organizational chart, but it draws a picture of flexible authoritative submission. *The president moved the chair at the direction of the janitor.*[40] Organization is submission, and submission is service. The Rotarians have an excellent slogan: "He profits most who serves best." If you love me you'll do what I want you to do. Love is authority from the bottom up.

Pain from the Top Down

In a recent book Clyde Reid talks about "leaning into your pain."[41] Find the spot where life hurts you and let your weight down on it. Don't lean *away* from your pain, lean *into* it. In submission your pain is accepted—you open your arms and let the weight of your pain support you: God is in your pain. "Jesus set his face like a flint for Jerusalem":[42] He leaned into his pain. Perfect love, says Kierkegaard, is loving the one who makes you miserable. Christian leadership leans down into its pain.

I write now—scribbling—on a Delta Airlines flight into Washington, D.C. Beneath us the Shenandoah Valley of Virginia peeks up from underneath almost closed eyelids of gray clouds. We will land soon. Two black men sitting in the seats behind me have been talking. I am their neighborly eavesdropper. I surmise them both to be deep in black strategy on the racial crisis, perhaps on a civil-rights-group staff. A moment ago one of their exchanges struck me:

"The South might wind up being freer than the North."

"Yes. It might."

I sit cogitating. Blacks more free in the South? Is he correct? If he is I know one reason why. Black men in the South own a legacy of submission. It is the Negro's national heritage. Their influence on us all today—politically, educationally, musically, artistically, culturally, athletically, religiously—their influence sprang from their submission. Blacks constitute only 11 percent of our national population. Yet in moral authority that 11 percent leaves any other 11 percent in the country dwarfed. It dominates the national landscape. We white men have been out-suffered.

Our plane just landed at National Airport. The two men behind me have stood up now, got their gear, and walked out of the plane. What handsome fellows! I wish I knew them better—it would do me good. That second one just put on his raincoat. Hmm. I forgot mine. Outside it's a flood. Rain in Washington reassures me about who's in charge. Heaven weeps. Earth grows green from heaven's tears. Pain from the top down is the way things are.

Leaders don't have to manufacture pain. You've got it everywhere around you. Self-flagellation is only running away from authority pain that is real. Mr. Nixon—or any other leader—can't afford self-pity. Presidential pain means only that you're president. In Christ you submit to your pain. You accept it. You thank God he is in it. You consciously—smack dab to its face—you consciously rejoice that at Calvary your pain has been whipped.

My taxi ride from downtown Washington out to the airport— Dulles International—illustrates. (Not much time to write during my stay up there. I'm scribbling again—now on Braniff back to Texas.) It was an incandescent taxi ride. My cab driver—a Negro —started talking; I kept asking questions. Just past the Washington Monument he got going—this forty-nine-year-old dark-black-skinned Washington native with the white pork-pie hat, brim turned down around his face, really got going telling me about his fifteen-year-old son. Three years ago the boy—dissatisfied with his public school—asked could he go to a prep school in New York. To humor the eager boy on this passing whim the Dad agreed to finance an entrance examination—$100—sure his son would fail

—"80 percent of the white kids fail." But—you've heard about mixed emotions—the boy passed! The annual tab? $3,500 plus extras! So my cab driver says, "I work for the government regular, but here I am driving this cab two days a week and most nights! I moonlight, I daylight, I'm lookin' for any other light I can find!"

"Why?" I ask him, "Why do you do it?"

"Well," he says, "it's a matter of your values. One of my friends wanted to know what I was trying to do, sending my son to an uppity school. I told him he could spend his money on Cadillacs and cigars if he wanted to but to me it was just so much bravado. He really made me mad. I guess I embarrassed him. He didn't speak to me for a month! I'm investin' in my son. People nowadays want 'instant black man' but it don't work that way. Education is like two men goin' across the desert carryin' water buckets. Education decides how deep in your bucket is the water level. I only got to the seventh grade myself: it was stay in an' starve or come out an' eat. My people were slaves. Cotton was king: up an' down those rows-in-the-sun; I know how to work. I know how to be a servant. . . ."

I couldn't believe my ears. His words tumbled out in a torrent. I broke in telling him what I had just written. It spurred him on. "I told my son that regardless of what happens if you keep segregation or prejudice or resentment in your heart you're racing with a log on your back. I don't care if you're purple, blue, black, pink, or chartreuse. I live in the richest country in the worl', I was born in the capital of the richest country in the world. I was born in poverty, obscurity, misery, an' stench. But I got me a split-level house; I got me pink bathrooms an' blue bathrooms an' an all-'lectric kitchen with the range built in flush with the sink. I can't change the world an' I can't change all black people. But I sure can change that part of the world where I'm responsible."

It was hard to write down on the back of my ticket envelope all I was hearing. Just before the cab got to Dulles he told me about the boy, their church, and the handbell choir. Christian leadership is your own commitment to your own particular suffering: you lean down into it. Pain from the top down makes for power from the bottom up. I'd like to meet that cab driver's son.

Submission to Whom?

Are you bothered by this talk about submission? Does it conjure up for you a tyrant stepping on a slave, smushing him under his heel? I have before me a letter from a friend. He is afraid my book will be exploited by law-and-order extremists, twisted and turned by right-wing politics, used falsely defending the status quo. I thank him for his concern; truth will win out: to speak is to be misunderstood. Christian submission does not cater to tyranny: it destroys it. (1) You submit "in the fear of God"; (2) you gain holy authority; (3) freedom flourishes in order; (4) true liberty is obedience; (5) you also "resist the devil."[43] Submission to Christ's authority could have saved Europe. "Good Germans"—a nation knuckling under to Hitler—had not been on any kick of submissive authority, you can bet your hobnailed boots. Never forget that the Nazis arose—in the Weimar Republic's constitutional democracy—as a move of right-wing revolution. Discriminate. Submission fearing God *fights against* submission fearing man. Einstein said it took the Nazis to make him appreciate the Church; he hadn't before. Christianity, as Chesterton said, has not been tried and found wanting, it has been found difficult and not tried.

What Christ offers is the conversion of Establishments. We call Matthew 28:18–19 the Great Commission: "All authority in heaven and on earth has been given to Me. Go therefore and make disciples of all nations, baptizing them in the name of the Father and of the Son and of the Holy Spirit." (1) Notice Christ used the word "nations." Not just individuals alone: structures, governments, institutions—nations. Every family is a nation. Every corporation is a nation. Every labor union is a nation. We are a nation of nations. (2) Notice the word "authority." He tied the whole process to the kind of universal cosmic authority given in his resurrection from death at the hands of human tyranny and rebellion. (3) Notice the word "name." Not "in the [plural] 'names' of the Father, Son and Holy Spirit," but "in the [singular] 'name' " of the God who is the Trinity. The God of all real relationships, the God of all good organization, the Spirit of the Father and the

Son: the triune One. "In Christ all nations are blessed."[44] We baptize, we saturate, we immerse the structures in the organizational style of tomorrow.

Submission to whom? Secular sociologists have studied extensively on *leadership perception*. They say three standards will enable you—in any situation—to perceive a man's leadership potential: (1) his perceived competence, (2) his identification with the group, (3) his personal characteristics.[45] Each standard points you to Christ. His competence, his cross, his character. Christ's leadership is secure; two thousand years only make it more clear. He *is* humanity's leader; no challenge can alter that fact. His enemies fight without risking honest attack or open comparison. They falsify, they confuse, they ignore, they question, they counterfeit, they deny. But they dare not confront Christ on his own ground, this ground of organization. Before the power of blinding submission they quake. Authority incarnate is Submission; Submission incarnate is Authority. "Mao Tse-tung says, 'Power comes from the barrel of a gun.' "[46] It does not. Power comes from the barrel of an empty tomb.

Submission to Christ! Submission is our inescapable way down because rebellion is our unrealistic way up. You learn your submission to Christ as you learn to submit to others. In submission you learn humility. No one else can be humble for you: "humble yourselves."[47] Rebellion puffs you up; submission trims you down. Trying to be God is your rebellion; agreeing to be human is your submission. Rebellion is you the balloon; submission is you the brick. Rebellion is monstrous glandular obesity compounded with bloating: the circus fat man sick. Submission is weight-control: the perfectly proportioned you. The meek you is the you of power: the awesome, terrible meek. Davis Yeuell says, "Meekness is power under control for the sake of another." Meek power! Leonard Holloway says, "Love is serving others without violating your own integrity." Integrity serves! Jesus says: "Blessed are the meek for they shall inherit the earth":[48] You are the humble Hercules.

How does it work? I call it the Church Principle: *"Organizations demand followers. Followers lead by serving their leader. They lead by serving; in serving they lead. Under the Spirit of the Father and the Son. Amen."*

In the heart of the crucifixion story in all four Gospels you see Barabbas. "It was Pilate's custom to release one Jewish prisoner each year at Passover time—any prisoner the people requested."[49] That year Pilate chose between God and the people, between Christ and Barabbas. Pilate's struggle with those under him—his leadership collapse—pivoted around this particular man. His abdication of his authority to the crowd came as he washed his hands of Jesus and freed Barabbas. The warning word of his wife's dream interrupted the scene with Barabbas. When he asked the crowd, "What shall I do with Jesus?" and they shouted back, "Crucify him!" then it was that "in his desire to please the mob," he released to them Barabbas.[50]

Who was this man? St. Matthew said he was a notorious prisoner. St. John called him a robber. St. Luke gave you more detail: ". . . he was thrown in prison for an insurrection. . . ." But St. Mark spelled it all out: "Among the rebels in prison, who had committed murder in the insurrection, there was a man called Barabbas."[51]* In St. Mark you get the drama. Barabbas was revolution's slave; Jesus was submission's king: He died in Barabbas's place.

1. Look there among the rebels—
    in the prison dark in chains—
    who is the rebel killer—whose bloody game is power—
    whose weapon revolution—his name it is Barabbas.

2. Tell me all about the man—
    his distinctions, what to note?—
    individuality?—no, not among the rebels—
    from rebels it's been stolen—
    robbing himself, Barabbas.

3. Just a mask without a face—a fist without a name—
    a spear without a soul—a forgotten Fidelista—
    an unremembered dungeon—
    who would have known Barabbas?

4. Then up long stairs they haul him—
    into the sunlight blazing—

*Most students feel Peter was Mark's main source; Peter openly sharing his failure in the story; Peter preparing to teach us the power of submission.

he looks, blinks, fights back the glare—
elbows shield his shrieking eyes—
"Hell's sunspots, Pontius Pilate?"—
the bewildered Barabbas.

5. He hears the shouting of a mob—
he fears th' cruelest tree—
"They shout so loud, they yell my name—
and cruci . . . crucify?
What does it mean for me?"—the terrified Barabbas.

6. Facts at last begin to dawn—
into his darkened thinking—
"A trade a deal a swap for me—
this man they call Lord Jesus—
for me His life exchanges!"—
bought by blood, Barabbas.

7. Calvary they nailed Him up—
Christ instead of Barabbas—
fist and spear and bloody mask—
Christ instead of Barabbas—
spikes and wood and crimson gore—
Christ instead of Barabbas.

8. "This man took my death for me—
stretched-out-there on my cross—
A new life He gives me back—
Never my old one again—
Rebellion died Good Friday—
Submission for—Barabbas.

9. Jesus died all rebels' death—
rebel below Him, betrayed—
rebels above, the tyrants—rebels down and rebels up—
Three days for rebels shrouded—all for you, Barabbas.

10. Submission or rebellion?—
two spirits fought in the tomb—
which one came out the victor?—
rebellion's still there, death's dead—
Jesus arose on Easter—Submission lives, Barabbas.

11. *Your* name it is Barabbas too—

and mine, among the rebels—
forevermore your life's a gift—
give Christ your thanks, accept it—
Jesus died sin's death for you—everyman a Barabbas.

12. In Christ you live by exchange—
not you, Another in you—
Jesus died there in your place—
You yourself not you but Him—
Christ alive within your skin—
Barabbas the little Christ.

The Ballad of Barabbas the Rebel gets support from two additional facts. One: "Barabbas," the prisoner's name. *Bar* means "son"; *abba* means "father": *son of the father.* Two: Barabbas had another, a second, name. What was it? It was "Jesus."[52] Jesus Barabbas—Jesus, son of the father. Jesus Christ our Lord died for all us human prisoners—sons of doomed rebellion—to reproduce within us his own kind of submissive power. Every day we all decide: Saul or David—the old extinct Barabbas or the new submissive Christ?

Let's critique. We have looked at Authority and Submission so far (1) in my own experience (2) in the living Original (3) up on top (4) underneath. The next obvious questions are when to command and when to obey, when to lead and when to submit, when to assert and when to yield. Paul Tournier calls these decisions *"to resist or to surrender."* The rest of our book deals with these how-to-do-it questions. We are out to "think Christ's thoughts." He faced these same problems. "If you love me you'll do what I want you to do." People around him felt just that same way then. Sometimes he responded Yes, sometimes No. I call it His Pattern Mark Ten.

Twice in the 10th chapter of St. Mark, as Jesus talked with different people, he said, "What do you want me to do for you?" Whenever Jesus could he would submit—to communicate love, to meet their needs—yet always he maintained his integrity. His unearthly authority came through to them by means of his perceptive submission. He was *always* submissive to the Father; he was submissive to human need *as* his obedience to his divine-human limitations allowed him to be. Jesus never calculated—as confused thinking does today—that "the need is the call." The need is never the call; only the call is the call. Our response to needs varies with our individual obedience. Jesus didn't heal everybody during his earthly ministry; his response to their needs was selective obedient wisdom. He did not run himself ragged.

Mark Ten shows you a Yes and a No. The first time, Jesus asked his disciples James and John, "What do you want me to do for you?" they said, "Grant us to sit, one on your right hand and one on your left, in your glory."[53] Jesus told them No. Shortly afterward, Bartimaeus, a blind beggar, cried out to Jesus for mercy. Jesus stopped and said, "What do you want me to do for you?" He said, "Master, let me receive my sight."[54] Jesus told him Yes. In both cases Jesus was dealing with illness. Bartimaeus had a simple problem—physical blindness; he knew he needed (1) mercy and (2) mastery. He presented Jesus no difficulty. Jesus could answer with a glad, simple Yes. With James and John it was different. Here was the most deepseated personality disorder—one Bartimaeus would face later—one I know a lot about myself—the problem: ambition, aggression, rivalry, competition. Jesus could not answer Yes. He had to answer No. But it was a No full of love —a clear statement about his own human limitation and about his authority as service. He listened, he took them seriously, but he told them No. James and John needed the lessons of self-love given away; authority and submission; the painful power of the cross. Jesus' No helped them to learn well later. A patient No is better than an irresponsible Yes. Jesus practiced the wisdom of Proverbs: "Faithful are the wounds of a friend—profuse are the kisses of an enemy. . . . He who rebukes a man will afterward find more favor than he who flatters with his tongue."[55] Love often says No. In this next chapter we find out how you decide when to say it. We don't have all the answers yet, but at least we're asking the right questions. Authority can be therapeutic or demonic. Submission can be therapeutic or demonic too.

V

The White Flag of Victory

*He emptied himself, made himself a slave. . . . Therefore God raised
him high. . . .
Philippians 2:7, 9*

Politics, power, and the Damascus Road: Tyrannical Authority
has produced few portraits more lurid than the early church's
persecutor, the Jew from Tarsus, the unconverted Saul. The risen
Jesus chose, changed, and captivated a tutor in tyranny. Christ
turned him into St. Paul, a picture of Pastoral Authority for you.

Last night I read politics—excerpts from *August 1914*, Alexander Solzhenitsyn's novel about pre-revolutionary Russia. Michael Glenny, Solzhenitsyn's translator, says the book's

> intention is to reveal a people to itself; and its significance is
> . . . universal. Russia has lived through such colossal upheavals in
> this century, has suffered so much, has so often been the battlefield
> of militant ideologies, has seen the noblest ideals perverted and
> debased, has forced so many tragically insoluble moral dilemmas
> upon her people, that no reasonably intelligent Russian can avoid
> going through life haunted by dread questions. What has it all been
> for? Need it have been like this? What can possibly justify the
> violent deaths of tens of millions of Russians in fifty years? Is there
> any sense in our history? Where did it all go wrong? Why are we,
> of all people, doomed to exchange one despotism for another in
> seemingly unbroken succession?[1]

Here in America in 1972 I write as the McGovern-Nixon cam-
paign is upon us. From the Right you hear shrill voices: a commentator condemns Jane Fonda's trip to Hanoi—"there is such a
thing as too much freedom"—neglecting to rejoice in a system
that gives her freedom to go. From the Left you see populist
planning—"a fortuitious collection of the dissatisfied"—nega-

tion's war on the "big-money boys" and the "crooked politicans."
Theology is politics too. Hannah Arendt says: "Every single organized group in the nontotalitarian society is felt to present a
specific challenge to the movement to destroy it. . . . what binds
these men together is a firm and sincere belief in human omnipo-
tence."[2]

> Their most conspicuous external characteristic is their demand
> for total, unrestricted, unconditional, unalterable loyalty of the
> individual member. . . . If totalitarianism takes its own claim
> seriously, it must come to the point where it has "to finish once
> and for all with the neutrality of chess," that is, with the autono-
> mous existence for any activity whatsoever. The lovers of "chess
> for the sake of chess," aptly compared by their liquidator with the
> lovers of "art for art's sake" are not absolutely atomized elements
> in a mass society. . . . From the point of view of totalitarian rulers,
> a society devoted to CHESS FOR THE SAKE OF CHESS is only in degree
> different and less dangerous than a class of farmers for the sake of
> farming. Himmler quite aptly defines the SS members as the new
> type of man who under no circumstances will ever "do a thing for
> its own sake." The watchword of the SS as formulated by Himmler
> himself begins with the words: "There is no task that exists for its
> own sake". . . . Totalitarian movements are mass organizations of
> atomised, isolated individuals.[3]

Totalitarianism gives you no rational way of doing things together
. . . except as master and slave. Totalitarian governments arise
from masses of individuals who have become powerless.

Totalitarian Saul or Paul the Pastor?—leadership's two styles.
His name before Christ was "Saul": he was named for the rebel
king. After Christ his name was "Paul": the name "Paul" means
small or *little*. What was Paul's power? "Almighty meekness": he
was humble.[4] Submission was power: Humility gave Paul an inward authority. How can we humans find unity, yet still keep
our multiplicity? Have you read Philippians 2 recently? From
Roman imprisonment Paul wrote to the church he founded ten
years before in Philippi. He illustrated Pastoral Authority: (1) Its
style: "Never act from motives of rivalry or personal vanity,
but in humility. . . ."[5] (2) Its source: "out of your life in Christ

Jesus . . ." (Paul describes our Lord's submission and authority).[6]
(3) Its succession: "So then, my friends, as you always obeyed me
when I was with you, it is even more important that you obey me
now. . . ."[7] The transition is unmistakable. Paul describes Christ's
authority, and then—immediately—in an unbroken sequence of
logic following: "as you always obeyed me." Christ's authority
gave authority to Paul! Of his authority Paul had no doubt; he
exercised it decisively and continuously. Philippians 2 gives two
further examples of Paul's power in the life and work of his
subordinates: "I hope to send Timothy to you soon. . . . I feel also
I must send our brother Epaphroditus. . . ." This is no namby-
pamby egalitarianism, no wishy-washy "leaderless group"—Paul
had a magnificent sense of command. Slave to Christ acting like
a general! He showed us leadership up close; he was in charge and
knew it: his power to lead breathed strength. "Oh, but that was
Paul," you say, "that was Paul, that wasn't me, he was an apostle,
I'm just an ordinary Christian, I couldn't, no, not really, no, not
me. . . ." Listen to him in the same Epistle later on: "Follow my
example. You have us for a model; watch those whose way of life
conforms to it. . . . The lessons I taught you, the tradition I passed
on, all that you heard me say or saw me do, put into practice. . . ."[8]

Authority—an inner quality from Christ to you and through
you, whether you acknowledge him or not—arrives in two inter-
related ways. (1) Other people give authority to you. Sometimes
physically, as when your children are born. Sometimes politically,
as when you get elected. Sometimes economically, as when you
pay my check. Authority comes to you from others accepting it.
(2) God gives authority to you—legitimate, latent, potential, inherent, true authority—God gives authority to you whether others
accept it *or not*. Embattled authority is real—if it is committed
to Christ. Authority beseiged—in Christ—remains secure. You
act on it in obedient wisdom, regardless. Not fear, but love is its
power: Inherent Authority . . . in your home, on your job, in your
group. To assert the authority Christ has given you is your responsibility. Whether others accept it is their responsibility, not yours.
Both (1) and (2) are authority from God: you assert your leader-

ship in the wisdom of obedient love. Because they *did* accept Paul's authority, Philippi was a happy church, full of joy. "Rejoice" appears eleven times and "joy" six times in Philippians, more than in any other of Paul's Epistles. Corinth was an unhappy church, full of pain. They fought over Paul's authority: rejecting Paul they rejected Christ. Party-spirit, immorality, disorder in the Corinthian church caused Paul great suffering. He wrote Corinth about Christian consolation—they were making him hurt.[9] In Paul's ministry and life the issue of pastoral authority was constant. Who are you—who am I—to think it will be different for us? Authority accepted and authority rejected surround every leader. Over the issue of his authority Jesus' conflict came; we share the selfsame warfare now.[10] He says to you today that these conflicts—your pastoral authority tensions—actually inhere in your humanness. Christ suffered rather than deny his authority—Paul did the same—and so will you. Pastoral authority is the universal democratic authenticity of the Church—every member of Christ shares his Lord's authority. In a day of collapsing homes, schools, businesses, churches, and governments, Paul has a lesson to teach us: the lesson of pastoral authority, the lesson of *Christ in you*. Christian authority, whether it is accepted or rejected, has one constant: it flows from Christian submission. Broad-based pastoral power gives you healthy politics. Powerful individuals make a powerful society. The authority of the Lord Christ is the only alternative you have to enforced tyranny. Slavery to Christ is our only freedom. Either you accept the Ruler of Creation's right to your incontrovertible loyalty or else totalitarianism stalks you now, individually and socially—involuntary servitude. Paul shows us the new politics.

Adam and Eve and You

My problem is I don't want to be *little* like a man: I rebel to be *big* like God. The king of all sins is pride. No other sin runs it a close second. Beside pride—or self-conceit—all other vices are peanuts. Drunkenness, sex sins, greed, temper, violence: these are all gnat's eyebrows compared to the mountain of pride. Pride is the sin that made the Devil into the Devil. Pride makes you independent of God. Independence is the diametric opposite of worship. The two cosmic opposites are love and pride. John Milton described it in *Paradise Lost.* Satan decided: "Better to reign in hell than serve in heaven."[11] Authority-and-submission is pride's battlefield. Satan refused to be under God: he wanted to lead himself. Can you imagine the headlines? "Revolution in the World of Spirit!" "Holy Hierarchy Assaulted!" "Declaration of War against God!" "Satan Attacks the Most High!" Either you understand this background or else mankind baffles you forever: Man is God's creation made for love and friendship with himself, made in God's image; Satan pushed his civil war from heaven to engulf the earth, as God had known he would. Satan's strategy was to get into humanity the principle of independence, of revolt, of disobedience.

"Rebellion Spreads!"

Adam and Eve in Genesis is not a clever little story about a man and a woman and an apple and a snake. It is a divine exposé of Satan's plan to destroy God by destroying mankind. Revolution glorifies the snake. Satan's appeal struck at the heart of man's God-given leadership instinct: it only violated authority-and-submission. What did the Devil say to Eve? "Eat this and you shall be like gods."[12] First it denied our creation. They were already like gods, created in God's likeness. Satan questioned their self-image, implied they were not what they were. Second it denied God's goodness. Our Lord's commandments always produce happiness for us. (Automobile makers know how to get their cars to run!) It was insane—but fiendishly clever; it struck straight at our jugular; it attacked authority-and-submission: "Eat this. . . . Doubt God, question his word, decline his counsel, ignore his advice, forget his instruction, reject his command. Doubt God . . . and you shall be like gods." One little piddling disobedience and . . . *you can be the leader yourself!!!*

The rest is gruesome history, sad and cyclical. They bought Satan's story. They made the deal. They did not become leaders: Satan became the leader; they became blind followers. God still reigned, in control of his world. But estrangement, murders, wars, exploitation, bloodshed, and death captured humanity that day. Ever since then all us brilliant little human idiots troop in a long thin line, tied to the same stupid lie, toy soldiers taking turns at suicide: over the cliff we go, into the lake of fire. Ever since Adam, we run . . . contaminated men, all of us . . . bombed by rebellion's unscratchable itch. The dust of death has settled on us, the white ashes of revolt. Do you understand why your pride makes you want independence from God? You are infected with the dread fallout of cosmic revolution! You want, as I do, to run your own life, to call your own shots, to go it alone.

But to think I can go it alone is my ultimate dishonesty. I haven't been able to go it alone since I was a gleam in Dad's eye, a microscopic miracle in the body of my mother. I wasn't able to go it alone as a baby. I depended on others for milk, for cover, for attention, for life. I couldn't go it alone in education. I learned at home, in classrooms, in books, from others. I don't go it alone for marriage. It takes two to tango. I cannot go it alone in my work. I write this book for you. Who can go it alone? I'm a dependent creature: any other conclusion is a lie. Self-delusion. Blindness. Humanity is dependence. Pride is not just an unfortunate little trait and humility an attractive little virtue. My whole inner psychological integrity is at stake. When I am proud and independent I lie to myself about what I am: I deny my own humanity. Self-delusion—the Lie—makes me deny my own createdness. I deny the sexual union of the parents who produced me. Pride and independence constitute human unreality—insanity on its way to death. I deny the "facts of life." If sex hasn't pointed you to God already, start thinking about how you got here: you create children because you were created yourself. If you don't acknowledge God, ultimately you get left "pulling rabbits out of a hat." Jesus said the Devil is "a liar and the father of lies."[13]

Freedom to Fail

C. S. Lewis hits me amidships pointing out that *Pride is essentially competitive.* From Satan's refusal to accept the role of created spirit, from his germ-laden revolt to become the God he

is not, from proud independence rejecting gratitude and humility
—from Satan's rivalry you get human rivalries . . . to spoil your
relationships, you get competition. God the triunity is relationship; Satan the destroyer is antirelationship. Rivalry, like pride, is
the opposite of love—its social opposite, pride out in public. Pride
takes no pleasure in having something—pride's pleasure is in having more of it than the next fellow. You cannot say accurately that
a man is proud of being rich. He is proud of being richer than you
are. Intellectuals are not proud of being bright, but of being
brighter than the next man. A beautiful woman is not proud of
her beauty: she is proud of being more beautiful than other
women. Pride requires a relationship to pervert before it shows its
true colors. The Peruvian Indian expression for "pride" is "I
outrank others." My pride shows up in my competitiveness.

When our oldest son was three he got a football suit for Christ-
mas. The smallest size we could find was size 6. In it he was a riot.
The helmet engulfed him: he looked like Roger Staubach in a
space suit. The shoulder pads and jersey swallowed him up like a
tent over a midget upside down. Worst of all were the pants. They
were hopeless—until we remembered a gift from Santa: a belt, a
gun, and a holster set. We strapped the belt and gun around the
football pants, with the jersey tied down inside. He looked like a
miniature Dallas Cowboy—bloated. On his first run with the ball
his pants fell off. How can you be a football hero with your pants
down? Young Howard and I played a game of Touch that evening
in the backyard. The goal posts were the driveway and the fence.
Each of us scored well: the game seesawed between us. Then, as
we finished, I made like the Devil. I stopped him at his goal line
(the Boester's grape-stake fence); I deliberately kept him from
making his last score: 1–2–3–4 downs he got stopped cold. The
game was over; the father defeated the son; I'm glad God forgives
competitive daddies. That night at dinner his frustration boiled
over. He pounded his fist on the table, screaming and crying: "It's
stupid not to win; it's stupid not to win!"

He was right. It is stupid not to win. (It's even more stupid not
to let your children win.) Losing makes you feel small. Nobody
likes to lose; the reason we try to win is we hate being small: I am

small so I act as if I were big. I live behind giant-sized masks pretending I am an invincible winner, pretending I am big. I drop the names of prominent people so you are impressed with my importance. It makes me look bigger. I brag about my achievements—not openly, subtly—I don't want you to think I'm a braggart, I want you to think I'm big . . . bigger than you. I put you *down* because I'm desperate to get built *up*. Like Mark Twain I arrange to discharge my obligations so the report is heard for miles around. It's the reason why I use so many masks: The game is "movable masks." In a religious group I shove up my religious mask, combination John Wesley, St. Francis and Father Divine. In a business group I use my business mask: John Hartford, Paul Getty, and Colonel Sanders. Most often I use my "great-guy" mask: Arnold Palmer, Groucho Marx, and Mr. Clean. But these masks are bigger than anything I was built to carry: as I juggle them they're getting me down. My nerves, my ulcers, my insomnia, my weight, my anxieties, my irritability, my exhaustion: my masks are straining me. I've got hernias in my soul.

Pooped out on the treadmill of pride I start to think: "Maybe I'm not big after all. Maybe only God is big. Maybe I'm small." Montaigne said, "Perched on the loftiest throne in the world I'm still sitting on my own behind." Pride makes me look down on other people. Looking down on others I see nothing above myself. I see dirt and dust and pins and pennies looking down, but I miss the stars. A telescope with the big end toward me makes the stars faraway; a telescope with the little end toward me puts heaven at my fingertips. Looking down on other people denies my humanity; I try to be what I am not—God and not man. "Judge not."[14] I am not the Judge.

What about someone with *religious* pride? What about the conservative who is proud of his evangelical piosity? Or the social progressive who is proud of his liberal conscience? What about him? He worships an illusion, that's what—the shadow of himself. When my religion makes me superior to others, I have made contact not with God but with the Devil. I have plugged myself into the wrong socket. Like the Sunday school teacher who finished her lesson on the Proud Pharisee and the Repentant

Publican: "Now, children, let us rise and be dismissed. Let us thank God we are not like that terrible Pharisee!" Pride in church is pious hell. My travel to Japan taught me to learn from every man. Shintoism is Japan's ancient religion. Reverence for your ancestors and the worship of nature leave you with incomplete data on God: Shinto is theologically inadequate. "Honor your father and mother" is not worshiping them. God *in* nature is not the same as God *is* nature. But look at the splendor of Japanese esthetics and the gentleness of Japanese courtesy! How much they have to teach us—we who believe God created nature but neglect to see him in it, we who believe God gave us the family only to revolt against it. Several years ago Barbara Dan and I went with Billy Graham to Japan. The Japanese people ministered the Cosmic Christ to us at the same time we were preaching him to them. They taught us about God: their appreciation of order and beauty is superior to ours. Jews, Muslims, Buddhists, Hindus, or Heterodox Sectarians—I count you better than myself. "In my flesh there dwells no good thing . . . all my righteousness is filthy rags. . . . God be merciful to me a sinner. . . ."[15] Christianity is God's goodness in me by exchange. Christ's life in me—"Not I but Christ"—makes humility possible. Christ is Humility incarnate. I can walk through life with my pores open, ready to learn from Christ through everyone. Jesus affirmed Pilate, dying at his hands: "The man who handed Me over to you is guilty of a worse sin" . . . even at his death, boosting poor desperate Pilate up, explaining that religion determines politics.[16] Humility died for you and rose up: you can be humble without sacrificing your integrity. If I were further along exchanging my sins for Christ's goodness I could explain it better. When we are in the presence of God, says C. S. Lewis, if we think of ourselves at all it is as very little and very dirty and very small. Preferably, we will think about God himself.

I was conducting a university seminar once on "Christianity and Business." The professor who introduced me was overly expansive: he made our company sound like a regional version of Safeway, A&P, and Kroger combined. His extravagance triggered the class cynic. I could see the poison in his eye as this bright young guy raised his hand for a question.

"Mr. Butt, we've been told about your *big* company. How do you interpret Jesus' saying that it is easier for a camel to go through the eye of a needle than for a rich man to enter the Kingdom of God?"

When the laughter died down—from my ten-foot hole—I explained. "Rich" and "poor" are relative terms. My financial statement wouldn't bowl over an Aristotle Onassis. *A poor American is rich compared to an average man in India.* This obvious fact struck Jesus' disciples immediately. As soon as he made his statement they asked: "Who then can be saved?" And he replied: "With men it is impossible but with God all things are possible."[17]

How are rich men saved? Like everybody else . . . by the miracle of grace. Jesus was telling us our riches multiply the peril of our pride and independence. Satan's downfall was his magnificence. Both around and within me I see the risk of trusting, not in God but in money. But any kind of riches will do. If you are emotionally rich your security makes you feel no need for God. Intellectual riches can make you feel wiser than the Scripture. If you are rich in physical beauty, or athletic skill, or social charm you can be kept from God by your riches. Popularity, practicality, political power —all kinds of riches threaten your trust in God. Any kind of wealth will keep you out of the Kingdom if you love it more than you love Christ. "Blessed are the poor in spirit for theirs is the Kingdom of heaven."[18] You must be little, you must be poor, the only entrance into the house of God is the door of destitution. This repulses many people. Those wealthy in material things, in education, in connections; the affluent in emotional stability, in bureaucratic know-how, in moral rectitude: these people flinch to see poor wretches crawling into the Kingdom. The alcoholic, the dropout, the bored, the perverted, the embittered, the nervous, the timid, the impassioned, the lonely, the sleepless, the anxious, the sensual, the unbalanced, the guilty, the failed, the lost: these are the blessed poor. When they try to be good they find they cannot make it. They need Christ. For us who are lost sheep it is either the pit or the cross. Christ always ran around with sinners. He still does. Boy, am I glad. But for you upstanding moral people, you for whom a good kind of life comes easy, look out. Yours is the hardest case of all. The vainest people in the world are those who want to be considered respectable. You have a solid home and high standards and moral virtue: they are pinned on you like a medal. But still you have not surrendered your pride. Your condition before God is truly frightening. As far as natural goodness goes, remember the Devil was once an archangel. He was as far above us in natural goodness as we are above a jellyfish. There is no evil of which I am not capable. Potentially I am a drunkard, a murderer, a blasphemer, a robber, an adulterer. You name it: I could be it. Why am I not these things?

(1) I'm a coward. I'm scared of the consequences.

(2) I was reared in a Christian home, soaked in Christian culture.

(3) The sovereign grace of God. My foulest potentials are unrealized.

The one thing I cannot do about any of my virtues is brag. Any goodness I possess is not *me:* it is *Christ in me.* I have no goodness of my own: it is mine only as Christ's gift. "Grace" means unmerited favor. God's grace turns tables on my pride. If I achieve I am proud. If I receive I am grateful. *Works* is the path of pride. *Grace* is the path of gratitude. Humility is happiness. If I were more humble I'd be more happy: joylessness is a sin; the poor in spirit are happy.

Christ offers you the freedom to fail. Losing is not the worst thing that can happen to you—the worst thing that can happen to you is disobedience. Losing becomes irrelevant. "Losing" comes only from Satan, the Cosmic Loser—and since the cross, he is past and finished. "Losing" doesn't frighten you. Dean Martin croons me a sermon just now over my car radio: "I'm Nobody's Baby Again." He's singing a sad story of unrequited romance. His woman has left her man, his sun has left the sky: "My lonely is back, I'm nobody's baby again." But wait! He's in there fighting! Romance gets touched with Christian hope! You now hear Paul Tillich's *Courage to Be* in Dean Martin's baritone: "Even a loser can win!" . . . Pastor Roger Frederickson calls his book about authentic church renewal *A Church for Losers.* The word "succeed" has got twisted in our minds. In its Latin original it spoke of humility: *to go beneath or under, to follow after.* From *sub* "under" and *cedere* "to go": success is to come next after another, to follow; you succeed through your submission.

Now I can understand my three-year-old son and his edict: "It's stupid not to win." It *is* stupid not to win, if I understand that *I can win by losing.* "When I became a man I put away childish things": love means I grow up; I learn how to win by losing.[19] Then Dean Martin's prophecy comes true: I *am* "nobody's baby"; I've become a man. "Love does not insist on its own way."[20] I accept a realistic view of myself: I am a human, only a human, nothing but a human, but in Jesus Christ's deity I am a human all the way, in God's image full-grown, up to the hilt. I can accept being small. Love "vaunteth not itself, is not puffed up": love is little.[21] If we could see the cross as it was—without the sentiment of the centuries, without the aura of religious art, without the architecture of church towers—if we could see the cross as it was, I think what would strike us most would be its size. The cross was little—only big enough for one man—just one human-sized man. "Little is much if God is in it": God makes my littleness big. The concepts of "winning" and "losing" come to us in response to Satan's revolution; God is not competition, he is Being. A velvet-covered brick neither wins nor loses . . . he *is.* Reality never doubts Satan's defeat: "Before Abraham was, I am"; history reveals the Truth: God IS eternal victory.[22] Pride is your war against obedience, your winning or losing syndrome, your same old competitive trap. Humility is order and submission, preferring one another, your own willingness to lose. The Bible starts with a snake in the garden and God's defeat. How's that for openers? The Father lost in Eden so the Son could win on Easter. Victory is being—not winning—just being. Pride is the national religion of hell, the idolatrous worship of myself. Humility is realism, the way things are, realistic theological accuracy. "Paul" means *little:* bandy-legged, long-nosed, blue-eyed, curly-haired, knit-browed Paul, says his legend; Christ in Paul was deity in miniature; "strong when weak," content to be small.[23] All Paul's defeats turned out victorious losses: he gets arrested for preaching and is thrown into jail; he is so confident of Christ in him as Being Triumphant that he starts to lead his prison-group singing; an earthquake frees him from his chains, he doesn't run away; the flabbergasted jailer gets converted; all Paul's defeats turned out victorious losses. It happened in Philippi—*the little man* had won another triumphant defeat.[24]

Imitation or Habitation?

The first time I made an extemporaneous speech I ruined everything because I tried to copy someone else. I was fourteen, taking a course in speech at Corpus Christi High School. The classroom is still vivid in my memory . . . in the basement by the stairwell . . . I remember it as green, shrouded in black. I wanted to do something funny. I had seen a comedy sketch the weekend before at the movies. So I tried to reproduce it. From Andy Hardy it was great. On me it dropped dead. I couldn't have fallen more flat: not only did no one laugh—very few smiled. After that fiasco, only the grace of God could have got me back on the public platform. (Sometimes now only the grace of God can get me off.) It was my first attempt as a speaker to imitate someone else. I wish it had been my last. At various times since then I have tried copying Bob Hope's humor, Billy Graham's fervor, John Kennedy's eloquence, Douglas MacArthur's drama, Winston Churchill's phrasing, and Fidel Castro's endurance. But I have decided that while imitation is instructive, ultimately it only frustrates you. Rather than be a junior-sized Andy Hardy I'll be a full-sized Howard Butt.

At a deeper level the same principle holds true. The Christian life is not imitating . . . not even imitating Jesus Christ. "The Imitation of Christ," as Thomas à Kempis put it, may be helpful, but, alone, it turns out a dry run. It shows you your need for Christ himself; it performs the function of the law. "The law has been our schoolmaster to bring us to Christ": Imitation shows you your need.[25] If you really try to keep the Ten Commandments you soon find you can't. If you try living up to Jesus' "capsule commandments"—love God perfectly and your neighbor as yourself—you can't do it; you always fail. "What the law could not do, because human nature was weak, God did. He condemned sin in human nature by sending his own Son, who came with a nature like man's sinful nature to do away with sin. God did this so that the righteous demands of the law might be fully satisfied in us who live according to the Spirit, not according to human nature."[26] Christ alone fulfills the law: "What the law could not do in that it was weak through the flesh. . . ."[27] Christ fulfills the law in you: imitating Christ becomes futile; if Christ is only my example he is not a savior but a scourge. Christianity is life exchanged: the Christian life is not imitation, it is habitation.

Christ in you is a continuous gift.[28] The Christian life is not Howard Butt trying to be good; it is Howard Butt admitting he is not good. It is my confidence that Jesus Christ is good, that his death and resurrection were enough so he can live his life in me now by his Spirit. Christ in you; you in Christ: the ultimate human identification—"I have been crucified with Christ, nevertheless I live, yet not I but Christ lives in me."[29] You exchange your old life for Christ's newness. At this point, let me ask you a personal question. Is there somebody to whom you are important, or somebody who is important to you, toward whom your attitude is not good? Is there somebody you ought to love but don't? Maybe your father, your mother, your brother or sister? Your husband? Your wife? Your children? Your employees? Your boss? Someone else? You have tried, God knows you've tried . . . but these people are beyond your capacity to love?

Henry Parish, the teaching pro with whom I play tennis, is one of Texas' best. Henry married Dorothy Weaver, my secretary. At Ray High School, near our home, he is the coach. Henry and I play regularly; just as regularly I get beaten. The exercise is good; my tennis is not. I have always admired Pancho Gonzales—in his own time a tennis legend. What if, tomorrow when Henry and I meet to play, I could greet him with a surprise. Imagine for a moment that I could have Pancho Gonzales within me! Gonzales' speed, his power, his coordination, his shots! In me, not Howard Butt but Pancho Gonzales! Henry would walk on the court unsuspecting. On my first few minutes of warmup I wouldn't reveal

Pancho's presence. Henry would sag mentally: "Same old Howard. Ho-hum. No contest."

Just then, on my first serve, I'd turn Pancho loose. Wham! I can see Henry now, spread-eagled against the backstop! I can see myself . . . I'm beautiful . . . Smash! Forehand! Volley! Drive! Half-volley! Moving in! On the net! I'm gorgeous! Backhand!

Suddenly Henry snaps to. The backhand did it. "That doesn't look like Howard over there! It looks like Pancho Gonzales! The body looks like Howard, but I'd swear that was a Gonzales backhand . . . Howard's backhand?? Great guns! What's going on?"

"Henry, don't worry. It's not Howard . . . it's Pancho in Howard! And it's *preposterous!*" Of course. Why is it preposterous? Because Pancho Gonzales is *just a man* . . . and that's the difference between Pancho Gonzales and Jesus Christ . . . *Jesus Christ is God.* "I have been crucified with Christ. Nevertheless *I love,* yet not I but Christ *loves* in me." Trusting Jesus Christ you do what you cannot do otherwise . . . you love others as you love yourself.

Habitation—Christ's life in you; your life in Christ—makes pastoral authority contagious. You don't fear using your influence; you are not ashamed to be open: you don't preach yourself. "Be imitators of me," said Paul, "be imitators of me as I am of Christ."[30] Habitation produces Christ's life in you—worth imitating. You let Christ "settle down and be at home in your heart," and you finally become yourself, the "you" God created you to be, the "you" of power. The Christ who lives in you is the Christ who made you. You do not lose your identity, you find it. Christ begins the process of freeing you from your slaveries, the psychological bondages which imprison the real you. Movie idols—I was Clark Gable as a teenager, a blond skinny hooknosed Rhett Butler—movie idols usually replace some family idol—father, mother, sister, or brother. Teachers, sports heroes, intellectual, educational, or artistic models do the same thing. They keep you from being yourself. In Christ this process becomes conscious, out in the open, and self-releasing. Paul freed his converts. "Follow me *as I follow Christ.*"[31] Not little Pauls but little Christs: your unrepeatable genetic uniqueness in creation is fulfilled in the psychological uniqueness of your experience; in Christ you are you—the absolutely inimitable *free* and untrammeled you. I used to worry because "evil" people seemed more interesting to me than "good" people—more fascinating, more alive, more gripping. Pale, "churchy" people bored me; wild, "reckless" people charmed me: between an X-rated and a G-rated movie I'd have known *without checking* which would have been the most exciting. Now I understand my confusion. "Evil" people are at least *real;* I responded not to their evil but to their *reality.* It is easier to be really evil than to be really good. Real evil always whips phony goodness. Real self-centeredness is closer to God than fake religion. But self-centeredness, fake or real, religious or profane, cannot compare to the life centered in God: you come alive. Now I realize: my movie stars, my athletic heroes, my theater idols, my human "models" . . . it wasn't my own real life, it was *fantasy.* Imaginary evil is glamorous and colorful; real evil is dull and drab. Imaginary good is boring and monotonous; real good is adventurous and dramatic. If you sell out to Jesus Christ, I guarantee you, you will not be bored. The only way to *do good* is to *be good.* You cannot be good; only God is good: in Christ he offers to be good in you. The humble man is content simply to BE. The proud man cannot BE because he must DO. Doing demands masks to make yourself *bigger* than you are. My Clark Gable mask never did really fit; Barbara Dan says I do better as me. When I am proud I cannot enjoy the freedom of Jesus' "sparrow of the air," content to be a bird, rejoicing in what he is. I cannot enjoy the freedom of his "lily of the field," content to be a flower, happy just to be.[32] Humility is joy in the God who made you what you are, confidence that his plan for you is good. Pride forces you to follow someone else, your contemporary Clark Gable, your hero, your coach, your idol. Your self-control is gone: you are controlled by others. Adam was controlled by Eve; Eve submitted to the Evil Spirit: submission is not optional but inevitable—we will submit to someone, the only question is to whom. Jesus said everybody is a slave. He came to give us a choice: slavery to himself as freedom; slavery to anyone else as death.[33] Christian slaves—even when they are literal slaves —have always been free. When we give him our authority, God gives his authority back to us. We usually believe that men give us our leadership. It is not true—only God gives leadership to us. Jesus said, "Men's approval or disapproval means nothing to me. . . . How on earth can you believe while you are forever looking for each other's approval and not for the glory [the leadership, the authority] that comes from the one God?"[34] In Christ your focus shifts from man to God . . . you look to Christ as your moment-by-moment Master. You were made to be good. But you cannot be good on your own. Your efforts to be good only reinforce your pride. Religious riches keep you away from God more completely than any other kind. So you relax, quit trying so hard, and start trusting. Christ lives his life through you.

Question: Who is a Christian?

Answer: A Christian is a person in whom Jesus Christ dwells.

The Christian life is not imitating Christ: it is participating in his life. It is not what I do for Christ—my achieving. It is what Christ does through me—my receiving. Achieving poisons the relationship—I compete against the Lord. Receiving builds up my humanity: under God fully human. Achieving versus receiving: achieving is the life of pride through works; receiving is the life of grace through faith. Jesus lived his life this way; the Christ who lives in us is the Christ we imitate: Jesus said, *"I do nothing on my own authority. . . . it is the Father who dwells in me doing his own work."*[35] Imitation *is* Habitation. I am no carpenter-preacher in Galilee. That was the time and place of someone else's obedience. I am a groceryman-preacher in Texas. Christ is in me now but that does not make me Jesus. Jesus was his human name: Christ is his divine title. He was one human; I am another. He lived under King Herod and Governor Pontius Pilate. I live under Governor Preston Smith and President Richard Nixon. "What would Jesus do?" sounds pious and sentimental but it misses the point. My son Stephen gets tired of being the younger brother of Howard E. Butt, III. So he calls himself "Stephen William Butt: the one and only in the world." Through Jesus Christ so may we all. Texas is a long way from Palestine; 1972 makes A.D. 29 long ago and faraway: furthermore you are not Jesus. But Christ is in you, now.

The Discipline of Truth-Think

Christianity is emotional second; first it is intellectual: both emotion and intellect pivot on *will*. Christ wants my will. Intellectual and emotional problems are solved after I take the right step in my intentions. In each of us there are three little people: one named Intellect, one named Emotion, one named Will. Intellect has one vote about your relationship to Christ, Emotion has another vote. They both are cast after the deciding vote: the deciding vote belongs to Will. God never violates your will. Our Lord operates openly in the light; Satan operates hidden in the dark: both operate within the subconscious. God is out to make the subconscious conscious. For this reason Jesus Christ came in history, naked, uncovered, vulnerable to the Palestinian sky, dying in the hot Jerusalem sun, open—to win your will—your knowing, conscious will. God never forces open the door—he may rattle the windows, jolt the roof, thunder outside till the whole house trembles—but he does not touch the door. He respects your will, inviolate. He never crashes a party (unlike the Devil)—you must invite him to come. "Behold, I stand at the door and knock; if any man opens the door I will come in. . . . "[36] The issue is always your will. Intellect is hinged to desire; we believe what we want to believe. Jesus said, "If anyone wants to do God's will, he will know whether my teaching is from God or whether I merely speak on my own authority."[37] Your willingness to do what God wants you to do will determine your belief about Jesus Christ's authority.

Christ's life in you means for you to entrust him with your will as a habit. Christian maturity comes as this habit of submission allows Christ to operate deeper and deeper in your subconscious. Your intellect gradually—progressively—controls your emotions. You train your subjective reactions by the objective truths of the Bible. You learn the art of truth-think. How does this discipline work, to learn to think the truth?

You wake up in the morning. You feel lousy. As far as emotional or sensual or mystical "feelings" of the presence of God, you are a washout, a dud, a blank. Your head aches. Your stomach growls.

Your back throbs. Whatever your wife has planned for breakfast this morning cannot possibly be good. If there is a God, he is nowhere nearer than Houston. If he is anywhere nearer, then he is mad at you. You are internally aimed toward a day of misery and defeat.

What do you do? You pray. Deliberately. Consciously. Even though you don't feel like it, you pray. You exert your child-of-God authority to communicate with your Father. You assert your will; God within you is indomitable Will. You pray:

"Lord Jesus, I thank you for your death for my sins and your resurrection from the dead on the third day. I thank you for your ascension, your glorification, your outpoured Holy Spirit. I ask you to come into my life to fill me and control me now. Thank you that you do. Christ is in me now; I am in Christ now. Amen."

Your head still aches; your stomach still growls; your back still throbs. You may or may not feel the presence of God: it does not matter. God is secondarily in your feelings; primarily he is in your facts.

(1) Fact
(2) Faith
(3) Feeling

This is the unchanging sequence: first facts, then faith, then feelings. The facts of Christ's death and resurrection for you are rooted in history; nothing changes the facts. Your faith may waver, your feelings roller-coaster: it does not alter the facts. Believing objective fact frees you from the tyranny of subjective feeling. You are training your emotions to follow your intellect. You are submitting yourself to Christ's authority: you are "glorifying" God; you are giving him your leadership.

You will probably want to quote some Scripture to yourself to affirm these truths—your life's central, everlasting, unchanging facts. Perhaps Romans 8:1–2, or Galatians 2:20, or other passages of your choice. I usually follow the procedure of thinking consciously about God as soon as I wake up each day—when my head comes off the pillow—and reading some portion of the Bible before I read anything else. You may prefer some variation. But the kernel essence is indispensable. You discipline your mind; your feelings follow, concentrating on the facts. You are learning in experience about "the renewing of your mind."[38]

Is this self-hypnosis? No . . . it is just the opposite. Maxwell Maltz in *Psycho-Cybernetics* says our problem is to dehypnotize ourselves from all the negative self-images (the "not O.K." feelings) we received in childhood. We are "programmed for failure" because we were hypnotized in childhood with impressions about ourselves which were false. "Every human being is hypnotized to some extent," he says.[39] This hypnosis—this "not O.K." posture of defeat—is the consequence of the Cosmic Revolt translated into human sin, run through the generational filter of the family, then socially multiplied. Faith enables you to dehypnotize yourself. More accurately, God dehypnotizes you through your faith. God is the only ultimate reality: The cross and resurrection of Jesus Christ is "the only thing that ever really happened." In a world of phoniness and lying and deceit, you train yourself by the discipline of truth-think.

The consequences of this lifelong habit are incalculable for you. It was this kind of thinking that turned Saul into Paul. We have made the mistake of concentrating so much on the drama of the Damascus Road that we have missed its essence psychologically. The essence was not the blinding light or the audible voice or the smashing impact: the essence was the dialogue, the communication, the words. "Who are you, Lord?" And he said, "I am Jesus. . . ."[40] Remember, I told you earlier that sanctification— our turning from rebels into saints—is the process of learning who he is. On the Damascus Road, Rebel Saul's turning into St. Paul started. Christ's authority, Paul's submission. From then on Paul's battle was "bringing every thought into captivity to Christ" . . . "thinking God's thoughts after Him" . . . the discipline of truth-think.[41] Paul's own experience of a new way to think gave him confidence to say to a sad, defeated church like Corinth, "we have the mind of Christ."[42] It was the reason he sang in jail, why every trouble contained inevitable good, life as inescapable serendipity. The logic is (1) Christ's death and resurrection; our Lord is already the Winner. (2) Christ is in me; I am in Christ: we are united; (3) whatever tears of defeat I taste now will turn into the wine of triumph later. I do not fear losing; submission to God leaves me free to submit to people: the difference is in my thinking. "Those who live as their human nature [proud and competitive] tells them to, have their minds controlled by what human nature wants. Those who live as the Spirit [Submissive-Authority] tells them to, have their minds controlled by what the Spirit wants. To have your mind controlled by human nature results in death; to have your mind controlled by the Spirit results in life and peace."[43] You are calm, relaxed, tranquil *logically:* nothing can whip you. "All things work together for good to them that love God. . . . to be conformed to the image of his son. . . . Moreover, whom he justified, them he also glorified."[44] Your leadership is your glory.

Everything that happens to you produces your leadership, your authority, your power. God's management in you makes you a manager yourself. In a recent issue of *The American Scholar,* John P. Sisk discusses our "Rage . . . 'because we have not learned to manage frustration.' " Pride shows up in our frustrations; God is running the world, therefore we are not. We have not yet accepted the facts. Professor Sisk says, "The inability to manage one's impulses, the sense of oneself as helpless against interior forces, is itself enraging for many personalities, although the likely thing is that they will locate the enraging cause outside themselves— perhaps in parents or teachers who, by having failed to help them learn how to manage themselves, have in effect left them naked to adversity. Ideological hunger is ultimately hunger for management, an appetite that fascism has a great capacity to feed."[45] There is never any virtue in obedience per se. (Unthinking obedience was one of the problems in Japan.) Universally our difficulties have been in obedience to the *wrong* authorities. Healthy submission to people can proceed only from healthy submission to God. Submission to people without submission to God becomes demonic. Nazi Germany gives you a political example—as well as the grandmother around the corner from you now, tyrannizing her adult children—their family strife is incipient politics. Obedience is good *only* if it means subjection to Christ or someone he has

told you to be in subjection to. Grandmothers running their children's homes don't fall into that category: "for this cause shall a
man *leave* his father and his mother and cleave only to his wife."[46]
Christ gives you authority to leave . . . psychologically or physically. Authority widespread is the essence of democratic freedom;
powerlessness widespread is the essence of totalitarianism. Sometimes in exercising your authority you are accused of rebellion.
The authorities—the Establishment—in Jesus' day thought, probably sincerely, that he was a revolutionary. They were unable to
see their own tyranny as rebellion on top. Exercising your authority may cost you accusations of rebellion—it happened to Jesus
and the New Testament church both. A life of obedience to God
means we search our hearts to follow the Truth. Only God knows
what is a righteous assertion of authority and what is a demonic
manifestation of revolt. God is the judge of your fellow man, from
hippies to hard hats, you are not: judge yourself . . . "Examine
yourself. . . . if we would look at ourselves critically, we would not
be judged."[47] Accept your human limitation. Assert where God
tells you to assert; submit where God tells you to submit—the
need is for clear thinking. I remember one leader under whom I
found myself working in a service organization. I got called on by
God to assert my authority; I presume this man, our leader, saw
it as rebellion, and we two then had fantastic conflict. And yet I
refused to take the steps required to win . . . only to live in
day-by-day obedience to God, accepting also my submission to this
man. It was very sad. For its ultimate purposes the organization
we were in was finally destroyed. He never understood my strategy
of submission. He only feared my assertion of authority. One day,
out of the many on which we discussed our conflicts, he said to
me: "Howard, I recognize no authority over me other than God
Almighty!" I should have known that day he would not trust me;
he had no doctrine of Christian submission: Pastoral authority he
could not accept. He suffered; I suffered: but the organization was
killed.

Paul or Caiaphas: this is your choice.

Why was Jesus crucified? Authority and Submission: they rejected his authority. The men who crucified Jesus feared losing

their authority. Submission terrified them; they painted themselves into a corner. Murder became their only way out. Religion forced politics: they took it to Pilate. Now, with our centuries of perspective, what happened? Those men led by Caiaphas lost the very thing they were working to keep—their leadership. Caiaphas rebelled; Paul submitted. Which man has most authority today? Pastoral authority is the only kind of authority that endures. Submission is never suicide; it never means your authority is wiped out: it only means your authority is willing to suffer . . . and grow. Management consultant Fred Smith says: "Humility is not denying your gift. Humility is recognizing that your gift comes through you and not from you." Authority came *from* Caiaphas; authority came *through* Paul. How this will work out for you in practice only God can tell: I cannot; it is your excitement, your drama, your great adventure. But it is the reason Submission can never be a rule; it can only be a Relationship. Power is always and only relationships; beside relationships there is no power. It is as true for tyrants as for saints: the iron discipline of the party—Nazi or Communist individual sacrifice—is a pale carbon of the Church's free authority . . . the authority of Relationship. The white flag of victory is the flag of Relationship Secured. Totalitarianism's pathetic plight is Relationship Imitated. Blind following of authority can never be Christian: Caiaphas counted on it; he got the shrieking crowd. Animal obedience is mobs following tyrants; unmanaged movements craving masters. Remember how St. John quoted their blind unbelief: "Surely our rulers haven't decided that this really is Christ! . . . Have any of the authorities believed in him?"[48] They took their leaders more seriously than they took God: animal obedience is the self-righteous movement; human obedience is relationships of trust.

How can you be humble? Not by trying . . . that only makes you proud. You can be humble only by looking at Christ. By truth-think. Paul's own desperate need for humility was the reason he wrote, "God forbid that I should glory, save in the cross of Jesus Christ our Lord."[49]

Me too.

What is *the work of God?* What would you say is his work?

Good deeds? Human kindness? Obeying the law? Doing your best? Being sincere? Are these the work of God? No. No. No. No. No. These things follow. Put them first, they foul you up in pride. " 'Then what must we do,' they asked him, 'if we are to work as God would have us work?' Jesus replied, 'This is the work that God requires: *believe in the One whom He has sent.*' "[50]

Truth-think . . . believing in the One whom God has sent . . . gives you chess for the sake of chess.

VI

The God of the Ordinary

And God saw everything that he had made, and behold, it was very good.
Genesis 1:31

I began this book about conflict between me and my brother. Structure—organizational structure—was our fight. To see he was right about it took me a long time. Yet now I don't begrudge a day of the process: I was learning truth-think in everyday, ordinary, dusty routine.

Christian growth is exciting because, unlike physical growth, it shows you God in your conscious will. On the physical level you grow a strong body. On a higher plane you grow a strong soul. Spiritual growth is not involuntary; it depends on God's working *within and through* your will. Some of us are like apples. God gets us in one big bite. Others of us are like onions: layer after layer after layer.[1] In the end all of us turn out to be apples and onions both: we have different kinds of beginnings but afterward it's one layer after another. Even dramatic conversions—one-big-bite conversions—turn out as only the start. Knowing God is a process. You couldn't stand it all at once. Relationships build themselves more slowly than tyrannies. Physical conception is quick, but the baby's development has just begun. Explosions never replace growth. The seed in shallow ground withered though it sprang up fast.[2] "Instant foods" from your supermarket will never replace gourmet cooking. Perfection takes time. "Instant" salvation turns out to be a fraud. The adjective Jesus used was "eternal." Your faith is a pilgrimage. How does it work on the job? Is God only in your BIG moments? Of course not: Christ's uniqueness is as the God of the ordinary, the humble, the down-to-earth. He becomes real "between Sundays."[3] He is an everyday Christ. How do you experience God everyday?

Moses learned in the desert, alone. No one else can learn this lesson for you. These are the lessons of the desert—the deserted place—the lessons of contemplation, the lessons of silence. Stillness is the price you pay to see God in your everyday affairs. "Be still and know that I am God."[4] Some lessons don't come on the run, in the blare of the radio, with the honking of horns. They come in the desert. You carry your place of contemplation with you, in your daily discipline: Jesus said, "Go into your room and shut the door."[5] Pascal said all the trouble in the world is due to the fact that men cannot sit still in a room. Find deserts in the middle of your crowds: Gethsemane was surrounded by people. If you ever feel you are in an unlikely spot for a revelation of God, look at Moses' desert. Sand blowing like microscopic hot hail. Sand in his teeth, sand in his eyes, sand in his soul. Little scraggly bushes like tumbleweed flying everywhere. Moses' job was to stay out in the desert with the sheep. *Stinking* sheep. If you'd been reared in a royal palace like Pharaoh's, that sheep smell would have turned your stomach. And, talk about galling, the sheep didn't even belong to Moses! He tended them for his father-in-law! The situation was sad, sad, sad . . . and strictly secular.

You remember what happened? One of those bushes—an insignificant little bush—lit up with the presence of God. It burned. Moses caught it out of the corner of his eye. He stopped. He turned aside to look—a very good move. God spoke to him when he turned aside. You too have turned aside, reading this book, taking time to think. Moses turned aside to see . . . a bush which burned, without burning up.

"Moses!" God said.

Then Moses answered: "Here am I."

"Take your shoes off your feet. The place where you are standing is holy ground."[6]

Under New Management

"Here am I." Moses knew where he was. Do I? For each of us there is a place where we are at home. It is that loyalty, that desire, that love where the inmost self settles down. One's deepest longings live there. Utopia for me would be my dreams about this place fulfilled. Hell comes to me ahead of time as I fear my dreams may never come true about this place. I live in this house in my heart. It is the home of my soul.

Where do you live? We must be ruthlessly honest or we will never know our real address. When we cherish honor and recognition we live on Popularity Lane. When I crave accomplishment and success my house is on Achievement Avenue. Women whose supreme value is their physical desirability locate on Attractiveness Drive. Men who thrive on great muscles and a handsome face make their address the Plaza of Physique. To be sharp, clever, blasé in the ways of the world means we lodge on Sophistication Circle. When I live for clothes, cars, boats, homes, my true location is the Thoroughfare of Things. My desire for moral and religious recognition means I live on Churchwork Corner. Thrills to lift me from boredom move me to Entertainment Alley. When resentment festers inside me I dwell in a haunted house on the Highway of Hate. Clutching my children, suffocating their individuality, chokes them out on our Family Farm. Climbing onto drugs or liquor, using them as chemical caravans away from my emptiness and failure, name my shelter Escape Hatch. Groaning under my problems and bemoaning my troubles, my lodging is the Subway of Self-Pity. If my overpowering drive is proving my masculinity I have settled on the Street called Sex. Too often though, I live in none of these places. They are too passionate, too committed, too driven. I like to float—wherever my boathouse drifts—along with the fog. Name my residence Purposeless Pond. The Firesign Theater says, "How can you be in two places at once when you're really no place at all?"[7]

Most of us don't know where we live. Not only do we not know where we're going, we don't know where we are. "Know thyself" was easy for Plato to say; it is hard for us to do. Jesus said, "You will know the truth and the truth will set you free."[8] Freedom demands the truth about ourselves. "Anyone who eats the bread or drinks the Lord's cup in an unworthy way is sinning against the Lord's body and blood . . . ," said St. Paul. *"Examine yourself. . . . "*[9] Only through the truth about ourselves can life become a sacrament. "Lord, show me myself." Will you pray that prayer? "Lord, show me myself." It can turn out to be terrifying. You begin looking at your motives.

How do you learn where you're building the house of your heart? Here are some tips. (1) How do you spend your money? Your check-stubs give up-to-date information on your soul. The house of your heart is where you put your cash. My motives show up in my pocketbook. "Your heart will always be where your riches are."[10] (2) How do you use your time? My schedule points to my address: my working time, my idle days, my spare evenings. We find time for what we want; what we want is what we worship. Your hours mark out your motives. Why do I do what I do? (3) Where do your daydreams go? Inspect your imagination: your hopes, your heroes, your castles in the air. What topics are easiest for your memory? The movies you watch, the books you read, the magazines you choose: you point to your soul's location with your freest thoughts.

Most of us move from house to house, from loyalty to loyalty, trying to get some rest, unable to settle down. "Our souls are restless till we find our rest in Thee," said St. Augustine. He said it long before modern transportation. American mobility is more than house-trailers and airplanes and pickup trucks. We are all spiritual transients; we are all "On the Road": in our souls we're gypsies.

Once you locate the house where you are living, what do you do? You turn it over to God—a conscious act of your will. Do you move out of the house? No. No. No. Later you may or may not; God will make that clear. It is his decision, not yours: you follow along; he will show you. Do not move out, tear down, or burn the place; that is a great error. You simply *give God your right to the house.* The valid essence of the house Christ intends to restore. So don't turn yourself out; don't bomb the old place; don't demolish the house: your sin must go but not your humanity. Christ came not to destroy but to fulfill.[11] You don't ever tear your house apart; you put it under new management. You don't forsake your house; you ask God to move into it with you. "That Christ may settle down and be at home in your heart."[12] Consciously, solemnly, deliberately you give yourself to God. It is a wide-awake decision of your will. It is not done in a moment of emotional ecstasy or sentimental religious outburst. It is a conscious choice: awesome, unforgettable, death-to-yourself. If you have made this decision you know it. Deliberately you have forfeited your right to your own life—in preference for Another. You may not know how you made the decision, or when, but you *do* know that the decision has been made. If you do *not* know whether or not you have made this decision, you have another step yet ahead of you. In Christ you make your commitment conscious.

It is not that we give up things, but that we give up ourselves. Jesus said, "If your hand causes you to sin, cut it off. It is better for you to enter life maimed than with two hands to go to hell."[13] What is better to me than my hand? With my hand I work, I write, I take, I give, I greet my friends. Cut off my hand? My hand is my agent for good, for strength, for power. Cut off my hand? Jesus is saying I face something more basic than giving up my sins; I must give up my goodness.

I had been a Christian many years before I understood how simple (but how devastating to my pride) continuing the Christian life is once you have started. I thought some "additional spiritual experience" was needed; some mystical "baptism" or "filling" or "blessing" which would make me complete. Now I know such an "additional spiritual experience" would have been something else to make me proud, something else to make me superior, something else in which to believe. What I wanted was relief from ordinary frustrations—family problems, vocational pressures, my inner moods. Since lots of this centered around Dad and the H. E. Butt Grocery Company, everytime I got in a period of stress I wanted to leave, to get out, to make some heroic sacrifice. Like King Saul I preferred sacrifice to obedience. One day, long before Keith Miller came to Laity Lodge as its director, he and I had a significant conversation. "I've been thinking about Christ in Gethsemane," Keith said. "You know what I think? I think lots of his pain there was having to give up his ministry. All those crowds to whom he was preaching, those sick folk he was healing, all those people he was helping—he had to give up his ministry to die." Not long afterward I was reading Oswald Chambers' *My Utmost for His Highest* when one sentence reached out and grabbed me: "Most Christian workers worship their work."[14] Motive again, motive in the ministry: *most Christian workers worship their work.* Gradually the truth dawned. I had (subconsciously) allowed my ministry to become a way to compete with my Dad. He was a big-shot businessman; I would compete, match, and surpass him—as a lay-preacher! He had achieved; I would achieve more! The one house I had never seen was "Churchwork Corner"! Independence, accomplishment, ambition, pride, competition, rivalry—revolution's fallout had fastened on my Christian service. I underestimated my own inner depravity; our capacity for self-deceit is unfathomable. The thing that keeps you from God is probably the best thing about you. It is the idol of your work, the coat hanger for your pride, the statue of your achievement. Who would think of a preacher worshiping his ministry? My weaknesses do not keep me from God. The thing that keeps me from God is my strength.

I will always remember the back bedroom in the main house at our family ranch in 1960. I had made lots of commitments to Christ before then; I have made lots of commitments since. But my commitment to Christ there, one spring afternoon in that ranchhouse bedroom, tied it all together. I gave God my ministry. I asked God for nothing except his life manifest in me. I accepted the truth that whether my work is little or big is his affair as the Master, not mine as the servant—I committed my will to that fact. I changed my mind about my own ministry; I repented of church-work idolatry: I turned from religious pride's insanity. As I finished kneeling beside the green-plaid ottoman, in front of its overstuffed armchair, I knew I had transacted business with God at a deeper level than ever before. The thought that struck me first was: "Why, this is exactly like my first step as a Christian when I was a nine-year-old boy!" Twenty-four years before I had begun with Christ: the simple trust of a little child. Now, a quarter of a century later, age thirty-three, I was making the same step again. Finally I understood.

My experience has been to learn that there is no "experience"; rather, that Jesus Christ our Lord is in all our experiences. I used to think, "Now is the accepted time, behold now is the day of salvation," was just a text for revival meetings and evangelistic preachers.[15] I know today that it is more; it is a plan for all our living. Every twenty-four hours that I live is the accepted time: am I willing to go on changing my mind in favor of God, committing myself to him *continuously?* "Just as you trusted Christ to save you, trust him, too, with each day's problems; living in vital union with him."[16] Will I live by God's affirmation? Will I go on as I started? He sees me completed now. "In him you have been brought to completion."[17]

God always works through your will. If you cannot say to God, "I want you more than anything in the world—I want you more than anyone or any combination of my houses," then at least you can say to him, "I *want* to want You more than anything else."[18] Sometimes it helps me to tell him: "Lord, I don't know whether I'm willing to do your will or not . . . but *I'm willing to be made willing.*" The commitment of my will is never perfect; only Jesus Christ himself is perfect. My imperfect commitments open me up to the perfect Christ. "Commit as much of yourself as you can to as much of Christ as you understand."[19] Vitality in your relationship to Christ awaits your choice, your decision, your intention. God respects you too much to invade your personality without your permission. "As you received Christ, so walk in him, having been firmly rooted and now being built up in him."[20] Walk, walk, keep on walking, step by step: the automatic habitual use of your will. Chambers put the Christian life in a formula: (1) conscious repentance; (2) unconscious holiness. Never the other way around.[21] You consciously repent; you consciously commit; consciously you use your will. In his desert, Moses consciously committed himself to God. Have you located your house? Have you offered it to God? Have you come to your desert? Have you come to the end of yourself? Out of your desert have you said to God: "Here am I"? When you do, "He makes the desert blossom as a rose."[22]

Commitment and Confidence

Does it frighten you to be told that if you believe in Jesus Christ you are a saint? Don't let it: it's good news. You don't become a pious creep: *churchy* saints aren't. We worship the God of *creation*. Nothing around Moses looked religious: scrawny mountains, barren desert, dirty sheep. Moses' ears were not filled with anthems or liturgies but with the wind, the sand, and the sheep's bleating. Moses was just a man on his job. A man doing his duty. A man carrying on. The bush was just a bush: a nondescript prickly bush. A bush is a bush is a bush. But, like some star out of the sky, the bush burned. Like incense on an altar. Like a perpetual fire. It made you listen: you forgot the sand in your ears.

"Moses! Start acting like you're in church! Take off your shoes! Worship! The spot you stand on is holy ground."

Your circumstances always constitute your sanctuary. Moses' bush symbolizes his commonplace life: ordinary stuff aflame with God. For each of us who believes, the bush burns today. All around us bushes glow. But we must stop, look, listen.

> Earth's crammed with heaven,
> And every common bush afire with God;
> But only he who sees takes off his shoes
> The rest sit round it and pluck blackberries.[23]

Elizabeth Barrett Browning names me: I'm a blackberry picker! After my commitment at the ranch I was soon back at the grocery company office. Of course, as a lay-minister, I had preached for years that daily work was sacred. But that word for me was still the word. In daily experience I needed the word to become flesh, to teach me to *be* the church in the world. For years I had kept two piles of mail on my desk. Like the Army intelligence agent who went into the priesthood. He separated his mail into two trays: one tray from his parishioners and other mortals, one tray from his bishops, archbishops, and higher; the first tray he marked SACRED; the second tray TOP-SACRED. On my desk the left-hand pile of mail was about the grocery business. The right-hand pile of mail was about my preaching. One day I was going through my TOP-SACRED mail when the telephone rang. It was Fred Smith, my management consultant friend who, along with Bill Mead, the Campbell-Taggart chairman, had helped my lay-ministry grow. Smith's jovial Tennessee humor always brightened me up.

"Hallo, Buddy Boy. What's going on?"

"I'm sitting here in a soggy mass," I said.

"What's the matter?" he said.

"I can't decide what to do," I said. I knew I had made a new commitment to Christ; that much was clear. But I didn't know how to follow up.

"Butts," he said, "you are sitting there like a ship in port. When a ship is motionless the rudder doesn't matter—the rudder is your will—you can do anything you please with the rudder but it makes no difference unless the ship's in motion. God never guides a stationary object. You need to get busy."

"What do you mean?" I said.

"Whatsoever your hand finds to do, do it with all your might," he said, socking me with the Scripture.[24]

"I still don't get what you're saying," I said. "My problem is I don't know *what* to do. I can't decide."

"Answer your mail!" he said. I was a notoriously poor letter answerer. He had hit me a body blow. "Answer your mail!"

I started in faith that day to answer my mail. It doesn't sound like much. It wasn't. But it was enough. I found myself turning down most of my invitations to preach. I found myself paying more attention to the mail about the business. The years that followed were my best years in the company. I took over merchandising then. I belonged to God as much in those merchandising meetings as I ever did behind the pulpit in a church. I never knew before that business could be so exciting. Conflicts became ministries: drama in the middle of the prunes. My burning bush had been there all along: the business mail was TOP-SACRED too.

Without these developments you never would have known the story behind this book. It couldn't have happened. I wouldn't have cared enough to argue with Charles about the company. He'd have led by default. And I might not have learned—in my guts

—the lessons of submission. The two principles for our continuing life in Christ are these: (1) commitment; (2) confidence.

"Commitment" is your repentance; "confidence" is your faith. St. Mark says Jesus' first sermon was: "Repent and believe. . . ."[25] Paul preached: "repentance . . . and faith. . . ."[26] Commitment and confidence are your repentance and your faith. Confidence means you believe the bush burns. Answering my mail was an act of faith; I believed God was at work in my actions. I had been wanting God to change my circumstances. God had been wanting, in my circumstances, to change me. All your blackberry bushes are full of God. Emerson said, "Every ship seems romantic except the one on which I sail." We are all ready to do somebody else's duty but we cannot see God in our own: God is under your nose. God gave you your duty as a place of worship. We want visions and earthquakes and thunder and miracles. God is in the immediate, the unnoticed, the commonplace, the ordinary. Most of us want to be used by God, but we want to select the surroundings. Belonging to Christ, we see him in any and all our old surroundings—haphazard. He drops us wherever he wants us—through our mundane, ordinary, nitty-gritty situations—unaware. You can't start fresh with God from anywhere except where you are now. Quit trying to run away. You cannot start from where you are not.

Faith is thanking God *before* you have any change in your circumstances. It is truth-think to change the real you, the you inside your clothes. Stop begging God to help you—start *thanking him* that he has already helped you through our Lord's death and resurrection. Jesus believed, years ahead of time, that the resurrection would happen . . . throughout his ministry he talked about "the third day." He was living by faith. When you stop saying "please" to God and start saying "thank you" then you have faith. Faith is the "substance of things hoped for, the evidence of things not seen": it is living in Christ-centered confidence.[27] All of us live by faith—it is no esoteric religious predisposition. You enter an elevator by faith—you trust the elevator, believing it will lift you up or deposit you down—it is an exercise in faith. You climb into an automobile by faith. You see a doctor by faith. You eat in a cafeteria by faith. Where is your faith? In God, in yourself, or in other people? You believe God is in your immediate situation *by faith*. As I sit writing I am inspired to practice what I preach. Tonight we go to Laity Lodge. I have had a long, hard day already. I am tired; my back hurts; I've got the blahs. Yesterday the blow of a big disappointment hit me; a friend let me down. The sting has sprayed acid over me all day. What will I do? Will I wait till I get to Laity Lodge, hoping its beneficent atmosphere will help? Condemning my family to the aroma of bile all the way there? No. I will not. I repent of my self-pity. Since when have friends *not* let you down? Jesus' friends did. Who do I think I am? "Lord, forgive me for my self-pity. Thank you that you do. The man involved I lift up to you; fulfill him in yourself: thank you that you will. I commit our Laity Lodge trip to you. Thank you that you are in it, filling it with love and joy and peace. Through Jesus Christ our Lord. Amen." I do not wait to *feel forgiven;* I thank God I am *forgiven already.* I do not wait for evidence my friend can change; I affirm God's power to change him *ahead of time.* I do not wait to "see how it goes" at Laity Lodge. I give thanks for Christ's victory *before we get there.* "To have faith is to be sure of the things we hope for, to be certain of the things we cannot see."[28] I'm feeling better already; I look forward to our trip; the blahs get drowned in confidence. (My back seems better too!)

Living in the Now

Strutting around inside me is a miniature Napoleon. Every person—every man, every woman—is on a quest for leadership. The question is constantly before me: How will I get my leadership? These alternatives face me: (1) leadership by proud competitive rivalry, or (2) leadership by humble individual service. Howard Butt's "old" human nature, his flesh, his self-centeredness, makes him into a tyrant—your rival—Napoleon Bonaparte Butt. Howard Butt's "new" divine nature, Christ's Spirit within him, makes him into a servant-king—your friend—not Howard Butt, but in him, Christ.

Jesus did the most ordinary kinds of jobs. It takes all God's power in me to do the simplest things—his way. Christianity is not a way of doing special things. It is a special way of doing everything. Can I talk to a woman as Jesus did? Or ask for a drink of water? Or cook fish? Or walk through my hometown? Or talk to my men? It is bosses and basins and towels and washing fishermen's feet.

The dusty pedestrian duties of life demand God Almighty in us. It takes as much of the power of God for me to go to my office and sit at the desk and talk on the phone—as I *should*—as much of God's power to go through my *regular routine* as it does for me to preach a sermon or write a religious book. An evening with my wife. A golf tournament with my son. An ice cream adventure with my daughter. A conference on financial budgets. I am not supposed to be a gilt-edged spook with wings making a holy hum: one-half human and one-half angel. I am supposed to be a normal, natural, down-to-earth human full of creation's practical Spirit— the 13th chapter of I Corinthians dressed up in mod clothes. St. Carlo Borromeo sat once with a group of his friends for a pleasant evening of social chess. As they played the conversational question arose, "What would I do if I had to die within this very hour?" The others described their actions if they knew that within that hour they should die. Borromeo listened. Then he said quietly that if death came to him inside that hour he would continue his chess game. He had begun it in honor of God, and he could think of nothing better than being called away in the midst of something he had undertaken in God's honor. Chess for the sake of chess: in Christ all things are yours.[29] "Whatever you do, whether you eat or drink, do it all for God's glory."[30] There's nothing very churchy about eating and drinking, you say? Of course not—that's the good news. Awesome news, but good news. Church is everywhere. Wherever you go you can say with Jacob at Bethel, "This is the house of God, this is the gate of heaven."[31] Ruth Graham has a motto over her kitchen sink: "Divine service performed here three times daily."

Truth-think changes the way you think all the time. You don't get there all at once. It's a pilgrimage, a process, a journey. Woody Brookshire, of the East Texas grocery chain Brookshires, gave me

his lake-house motto on a plaque. We mounted it near the door
we use most:

> Yard by yard life is hard;
> Inch by inch it's a cinch.

The famous A.A. slogan is "One day at a time." Alcoholics Anonymous learned that you don't get over destructive habits in one
spectacular, gigantic, supercolossal moment. You get grace in daily
doses: "one day at a time." Jesus said it. "Don't worry about
tomorrow, today's evil is enough for today."[32] With the sin surrounding you, you've got your hands full right now today: commitment is a regular habit. Who saves you anyway? Your own experience, your own decision, or Christ himself? Christ saves you, not
your decision. You make continuous decisions integrating all your
experiences, receiving him continuously. A.A. teaches us. I've
thought of calling my group Pharisees Anonymous. My problems
are more serious than drinking. If you get drunk and fall in the
gutter, someone helps you recognize that indubitable fact. But you
get stuck up in pride and never know it. So, honestly, "one day
at a time" is too infrequent for me—I'm worse off than alcoholics.
Every hour on the hour and minute by minute and inch by inch
—that's my need. Jesus put it, "Always pray and never become
discouraged." Paul said, "Pray without ceasing: Never stop praying."[33] The specific on the Gospel prescription is the same one
you see on medicine from your physician: "℞: Take as often as
needed."[34]

I have a woman doctor friend in Corpus Christi who is unmar-
ried. We were meeting with her in a weekly Bible discussion
group. One night she electrified us announcing her new decision:
"I have lived my whole life up until now either in *retrospect* or
anticipation. I either lived back in the past in my regrets, or else
I lived out in the future in my fantasies. This week I decided to
live in the *present.* I was over at St. Luke's Methodist Church the
other night. I went into the Ladies' Powder Room. It was in an
awful mess. Papers all over the floor. It looked terrible. An impres-
sion came to me quite clearly: 'You should clean up this room
now.' " (You would need to know my doctor friend to fully ap-

preciate this story. She is anything but the tidier-upper kind.) "And so I did. I cleaned the place up. And as I did—in the midst of my cleaning—I was overwhelmed by a fantastic wave of joy!" Her eyes sparkled. "And that's not all. This week I broke up with a man I've been dating for eight years! He and I both knew nothing would come of it. It was strictly the past. So I broke it off!" She seemed elated. "And you know what?" She paused. "Already this week God sent me a new man!"

"Today is the first day of the rest of our lives." St. John Perse says, "We have so little time to be born to this instant." *To experience eternal life you live in the now.* You thank God he is in you now, right in the middle of your current mess. An Extraordinary Life in your oh-so-ordinary situation: you give thanks for what he is doing, quiet, noiseless, unseen, unheard. I repeat: you may or may not *feel* the presence of God. The Christian life is *always intellectual before it is emotional.* "In the beginning was the Word," the original idea . . . "and the Word [then in the fullness of time] was made flesh". . . felt as emotion.[35] We live in a sensual world; we face no bigger trap than religious sensuality. If we have an ecstatic experience with Christ we are tempted to feel he is in the ecstatic experience rather than that he is in all our experiences. He is in your ordinary routine just as he is in your mystical ecstasies: he is the down-to-earth God. Do not wait for goose bumps to reassure you that God is near. Thank him that he is near regardless of how you feel. Goose bumps are acceptable if you get them, but they really don't matter; life cannot continue a 24-hour-a-day-7-day-a-week-52-week-a-year-on-and-on-forever-goose-bump. It would deny your humanity. You are flesh, not glass.[36] Human nature loves to create idols. John Calvin said, "The human brain is an idol-manufacturing machine." St. Paul said, "I am convinced that in my flesh there dwells no good thing."[37] Mystical sensations can be either of the Holy Spirit or of human nature, either of God or of Satan. Lots of Christians get mixed up worshiping their experiences: the idol of Christ plus their religious experiences. Thank God he is with you when the goose bumps go. Beware of spiritual lust. You are learning to live by raw faith.[38]

Christ Jesus himself has made you complete. You walk-out his life in you by continuity . . . dusty humdrum step by dusty humdrum step . . . patient everlastingness one step at a time. Isaiah wrote, "They that wait upon the Lord". . . they that *expect* from the Lord. . . .

> [1] They will mount up with wings as eagles,
> [2] They will run and not be weary,
> [3] They will walk and not faint.[39]

What is the build-up, the crescendo, the climax? Not what human nature would think. The climax, the end, the goal of waiting on God is neither (1) explosive inspiration (mounting) nor (2) periodic intensity (running): it is (3) unflagging patience (walking). Mounting up like an eagle and our occasional need to run both have one result in common. They call other people's attention to us. Not so with walking: you walk unnoticed. What is the key to a life of faith-filled humility? "They that wait on the Lord": those that live in waiting expectancy . . . "they shall renew their strength". . . more precisely "they shall exchange their strength." Commitment and Confidence—changing your mind and saying "thank you" to God—gives you transmentation: the mind of the flesh replaced by the mind of the Spirit; your rebel mind fading away, Christ's mind in you taking over. One step at a time, every two and one-half feet, your life is exchanged.[40]

All day every day I keep deciding—between Napoleon Bonaparte Butt, the strutting revolutionary tyrant, and the practical, people-delivering, God-centeredness of Moses, the man of the burning bush. Leadership is life. Colossians 2:6 says, "As you received Christ Jesus the Lord so go on walking in him." It is clear in English; in Greek it is clearer. "As you received," *hos oun parelabete* second aorist active indicative of *paralambano,* to take to one's self, to receive by transmission—"As you have already received so go on walking step by step in him," *en autoi peripateite,* present active indicative of *peripateo,* to make one's way, to make progress, to regulate or pass one's life. Our word "peripatetic" transliterates it: *walking from place to place.* Go on receiving Christ in all your places, in all your houses, in every step. The

Greek *peri*, around, and *patein*, to walk, give it to you graphically: you walk around continuously receiving Christ stride after stride.[41] Your name is Moses. About you is your desert. Your bush is that prickly problem kicking up dust right now around your feet. You stop and look. Always remember: "any old bush will do."[42]

We come now to our two closing chapters. I trust by this point I've made clear that Authority and Submission are not rules but a Relationship. Your relationship with Christ is given to change your relationship with people. In the first summary chapter, next, we will apply individually, for our personal help, what we have learned about when to assert, when to submit, when to resist. The Pastor Principle is inescapably individual. The Church Principle, in the final chapter, reviews the social, institutional, or organizational outcome. Three conclusions form the backdrop as we turn toward our positive wrap-up.

(1) All human government is tainted by revolution: on top, tyranny; below, rebellion.

(2) Christ came to change the organizational coin on both sides, top and bottom, into his own nature of Serving-Authority.

(3) For the process of change Christ calls us to: *(a)* accept the pain-filled possibility our Serving-Authority will be misinterpreted as rebellion; *(b)* accept the patient suffering our Serving-Authority demands in the transformation of individuals, starting with ourselves; *(c)* accept God's strategy as our own—rather than impatient revolutionary terror, patient evolutionary change.

Revolutionary philosophy is fundamentally irrational. It argues "man is good; his institutions make him bad." Yet it solves the dilemma by another institution . . . the almighty idolatrous State. Essentially it is an argument of competition: "Their" institutions (capitalism, imperialism, constitutionalism) are bad; "Our" institutions (socialism, communism, fascism) are good. It judges the sins of others; it ignores its own sin. Revolution fails to be realistic about itself. The history of revolution shows that its philosophers did not reckon adequately with human sin—an incontrovertible fact. Realism about our sins drove Jesus Christ to his cross. No other way in your organization could you get I Corinthians 13 on top. "Now abideth faith, hope, and love." Trust, optimism, and affirmation: faith, hope, and love. "But the greatest of these is love."[43] Can you imagine it? In your everyday, ordinary life— the-cop-on-the-beat, the-boss-on-your-job, the-professor-in-your-class—everywhere you turn, surrounded by love? It has happened; it is coming; it is here now!

VII

The Pastor Principle for Every Leader

Whoever would be great among you must be your servant, and whoever would be first among you must be your slave.
Matthew 20:26

You remember the Pastor Principle I first mentioned toward the end of Chapter 2: *"Organizations demand leaders. Leaders do not lead to lead; leaders lead to serve. They serve by leading; they lead by serving. In the Spirit of the Father and the Son. Amen."*

Splashed on the canvas of my mind is a picture of the middle-aged leader of a Boy Scout troop. He is running breathlessly across a dusty road. His pot-belly heaves and puffs and jiggles the web-belt buckle of his new khaki uniform's short pants. Under his flat-brimmed Boy Scout hat, he dashes up to a wide-place-in-the-road-filling-station-attendant in old faded overalls—a gas station farmer. From the farmer's tobacco-stained mouth alfalfa grass droops. It points down toward the one solitary old-fashioned gas pump, lonesome in the sun, its hose curving in an upside-down question mark. The Scoutmaster gasps, pink cheeks quivering:

"Did a bunch of Scouts come by here?"

"Yep. Shore did."

"Which way did they go? I'm their leader!"

In my mind the picture looks like a Norman Rockwell cover for the *Saturday Evening Post.* I guess maybe his lost Scouts became the *Playboy* generation.

Leadership is glue. Husbands lead wives, parents lead children, teachers lead pupils, bosses lead employees, coaches lead teams, doctors lead patients, governors lead citizens. The list is endless. Equality is in value, not in function. Our value is equal. Our roles are not. Every organization's life is determined by its intermixture of hierarchy and equality. Institutions can never be healthy unless you love God more than you love the institution. Organizations —families, schools, churches, denominations, businesses, and nations—poison themselves. Institutional relationships sour and die unless Christ comes first. The man responsible for establishing the priorities and maintaining them is the man on top. Every group —from your own family to the family of man—craves a pastor. Your institution gets sick unless you, the leader, love God more than you love yourself. Leaders crucified with Christ release resurrection power into their organizations. I wonder what sin cost that Scoutmaster his Scouts? Gluttony? Sloth? Pride? Maybe he got to competing with some other Scout leaders and forgot about his boys.

Leadership is Christlikeness. It creates relationships of love. Sin robs you of true leadership. Your enduring route to being a leader is Christian obedience. In this chapter I want to summarize and apply the principles we have been learning. All our interpersonal relationships—continuously—involve authority and submission. Our unfolding drama of day-in and day-out choices gives us three options: (1) to assert; (2) to submit; (3) to resist.

Resistance is actually the flip, reverse, or negative side of assertion: Satan produces its necessity. You *resist* the Devil by *asserting* your will. Your authority comes from the authority of Scripture— resistance is really assertion. You *resist* Hitler's tyranny when your authority as a free man is *asserted.* So your choices constantly are either: (1) to assert your own authority, or (2) to submit to the authority of others. Seven principles of God's guidance can help you. How can you know God's will? How can you get God's guidance? How can you know when to assert and when to submit?

The Word of Authority

God's will never contradicts God's word. Dwight Moody wrote on the flyleaf of his Bible, "This Book will keep you from sin or sin will keep you from this Book." In studying the Bible there are three stages:

(1) The Castor Oil Stage. The Bible is medicine: you don't take medicine for fun. You take it because you are sick: you take it even though it tastes awful.

(2) The Shredded Wheat Stage. The Bible is dusty and dry: it gives you nourishment. Your need for growth, to develop, to become the person you are: your routine demands food for strength.

(3) The Ice Cream Stage. The Bible tastes good: it becomes your dessert. "God's laws . . . are sweeter than honey dripping from a honeycomb."[1] The psalmist loved ice cream.

At each stage God's word shows you God's will. Awakening in the sixteenth century rode on the cry: *Sola Scriptura*. Today God teaches you the same way: you know God's will by God's word. Premarital sex, extramarital sex, competitive motivations, neglect of true worship: how do you know they're off limits? Because the Bible gives you your boundaries.

Truth-Think

The Bible gives you power to stay within your boundaries: its authority is your power. Scripture's objective promises offer you self-control over your subjective emotions. Christianity is intellectual first and emotional second, not because you need brilliance, but because you need self-control. Ignorant people often grasp gospel truth easier than the educated. (Pride keeps the learned man from humbling his intellect.) But even the most unlettered Christian starts intellectually. He *believes* that Christ died for our sins in accordance with the Scriptures, that he was buried, that he was raised on the third day in accordance with the Scriptures.[2] Faith is God's good news believed. *Sola fidei*, sixteenth-century awakening's second rallying cry, again teaches us: there is no substitute for the mental discipline of truth-think.

Truth-Talk

Truth-think produces truth-talk. We gradually are delivered from being afraid of each other. Knowing that I am secure in God enables me to be more and more secure with you. Your acceptance is not indispensable to my inner stability; your rejection cannot disturb my true self "hid with Christ in God."[3] I can risk being open, "speaking the truth in love."[4] Only in Christ can you *speak the truth in love.* Outside Christ you can have *either* "truth" *or* "love," but not both together.[5] Anger can drive you to blurt out the truth. But you do more harm than good to the relationship. And we usually "speak lovingly" in soft-soap, or flattery, or sweetness, sidestepping unpleasant truth. But Christ in you combines love and truth: what psychiatrist James Mallory calls "confrontation without condemnation."

Christ guides me by the word of the Bible and by the word of the Church. Church authority is God's word to me through people. It is not rules or restrictions: it is God's people speaking the truth in love. It is pastoral counselors, Christian psychiatrists, everyday confessors, my family, my friends, my co-workers, my employees. The Church through these people is extended out into my world. Submission to them makes my authority grow. My openness with these people is a part of my openness with God. These are the people with whom I have no secrets. They give me a great source of strength: I'm not a man; I'm an army. I still stand alone; "let every man bear his own burden," but these people "bear one another's burden" with me.[6] Do I always take their counsel? Of course not. The Scripture stands over the Church; the group under the Word: Christ himself is my only ultimate authority. But I make better day-in and day-out decisions when I let Christ speak to me by the Scriptures and the Church both. An authoritative Scripture produces an authoritative Church. Speak the truth in love to each other and you get more and more like the Church's one true leader. Vulnerability and openness to each other are what the Scriptures mean by "walking in the light." Step by step your life changes. "If we walk in the light as he is in the light we have fellowship with one another. . . . if we confess our sins he will forgive us and cleanse us."[7] Truth-think keeps on producing truth-talk; more and more you look like a pastor.

Your Duty of Enjoyment

Your "surprise by joy" is that the more you look like a pastor the more you look like yourself. The you of spiritual authority is the real you. Wherever did you get the idea that Jesus' cross was destructive, masochistic, self-immolation? Not from God. Never confuse Jesus Christ with one of these poor unfortunate fellows who sets himself on fire and burns himself to death for some cause. Jesus submitted to the cross only because he could see beyond it. Why did he let himself be killed? For his own happiness! "Who for the *joy* that was set before him endured the cross, despising the shame, and is seated at the right hand of the throne of God."[8] Jesus leaned into his pain because he could see its inevitable legacy of upcoming joy . . . his leadership, his authority, his power. In Jesus' motives there was no self-destruction, only self-fulfillment. His happiness included ours, which is the way he is. God's self-love teaches you how to love yourself.

Driven or Drawn?

Gnawing within me for years, unspoken, lurked the fear that if I completely gave myself to God I'd wind up: (1) either waving a big floppy Bible preaching somewhere on a street corner, or (2) going as a missionary to the scariest part of Africa. I couldn't think of two worse fates: floppy Bibles are for home reading, and please, dear Lord, I'm not even a big-game hunter . . . not Africa! Then I told him I was willing. Now I know better. I was doubting God's love. Suppose God did want me in Africa. How would he let me know? He'd make me want to go! I'd want to go to Africa so bad you couldn't keep me in the United States.

God works through your will. The further I go with Jesus Christ the more confidence I have in what I want to do. Every day I keep continually committing my will to Christ. Believing in him, I believe he works through my will. The will of God is not something you do: it is something you are. "God is at work within you, helping you want to obey him, and then helping you do what he wants."[9] Christ unites my duty with my desire. "Work out your own salvation with fear and trembling": that is my duty. "For it is God who works in you both to will and to do of his good pleasure": that is my desire.[10] Christ-control gives you self-control. You develop confidence in your own intuitive desires. "I delight to do thy will."[11] If you feel driven you are being tempted. Mark says, "The Spirit drove him out into the wilderness. And he was in the wilderness forty days, tempted by Satan."[12] Prickly, tense, compulsive reactions always warn you: the Gadarene was "driven by the demon into the desert."[13] God is in what you are drawn to do—your drawnness. Luke says, "Jesus was led by the Spirit for forty days in the wilderness, tempted by the Devil."[14] He was drawn to endure it so he could teach us. The Lord said through Jeremiah, "With loving kindness have I drawn you."[15] You commit yourself to Christ in every situation, thanking him he is in it within you, and then *you do what you feel drawn to do.*

Sugar or Salt?

Relationships of integrity are never easy. Don't let conflict scare you. Trouble is essential: Sandpaper for the saints; spiritual spit-and-polish. Your leadership demands conflict. "It was clearly fitting that God should in bringing many sons to glory, make the leader who delivers them perfect through sufferings."[16] The Christian life is suffering for you and suffering for others too. Don't be afraid of obedience that causes others pain. Oswald Chambers said, "Whenever we step back from identification with God's interest in others into sympathy with them, the vital connection with God has gone, we have put our sympathy, our consideration for them in the way, and this is a deliberate rebuke to God. It is impossible to intercede vitally unless we are perfectly sure of God, and the greatest dissipator of our relationship to God is personal sympathy."[17] Effectiveness with others is first, foremost, and forever the work of prayer. Then your truth-think produces truth-talk: you speak the truth in love. Sympathy and love can become opposites. We are the salt of the earth, not the sugar.

Who's in Charge Here?

God is in the structure. One God who is Father, Son, and Holy Spirit gives you structure: the Trinity is structure; God is structure's Author. Never ignore the organizational chart. When you ignore it you ignore God. "He puts one man down and raises up another."[18] Define the structure; leadership can't work undefined.

The Will to Manage

Has God given you leadership in the structure somewhere? Are you the family's father, the children's parent, the group's chairman, the organization's president, the department's supervisor, the congregation's pastor, the young's adult? Then be what you are—the responsible executive. Christ in you assumes the responsibility. Love in leadership means the will to lead. Servant-kings cannot escape being kings. Servanthood is the style, kingship is the role. You cannot make a servant-king out of a servant-suicide. You only kill the group. You cannot be the servant if you cease to be the king.

Marvin Bower's distinction as a business consultant lends weight to his words: "Long observation has convinced me that the primary deterrent to developing a stronger will to manage is the natural reluctance of most managers to discipline their subordinates or injure their feelings."[19] We fear conflict because we do not see ourselves as leaders. If you are the quarterback you call the signals. You hurt yourself if you do not. But that is the least of your failures. You hurt everybody on the team. A tongue-tied quarterback is a team paralyzed. Command is essential to social intercourse. Somebody's got to be boss.

The University of Michigan and M.I.T. joined forces in 1948 to form the Institute for Social Research. Its director, Rensis Likert, wrote the award-winning *New Patterns of Management.* He says, "The leader can never avoid full responsibility for the adequate performance of his group. . . . High productivity depends upon how well supervisors, managers, and the line organization perform their leadership."[20] David M. Ogilvy, chief of the Chicago advertising firm, tells about his job as a young man in a famous Paris restaurant under the great chef Pitard. He says, "I have observed that no creative organization, whether it is a research laboratory, a magazine, a Paris kitchen, or an advertising agency, will produce a great body of work unless it is led by a formidable individual. The Cavendish Laboratory of Cambridge was great because of Lord Rutherford. The *New Yorker* was great because of Ross. The Majestic was great because of Pitard."[21] Timidity fights leadership. Love takes command. Jesus Christ makes you formidable.

Love Takes Guts

Phillips Brooks' great book on preaching says the average minister's pastoral work "is pitched in too low a key. It tries to meet the misfortunes of life with comfort and not with inspiration. It offers inducements to patience rather than the stronger tone of nobleness. The pastorship of Jesus is characterized by its frankness and manliness."[22] *Paraclete*, the Greek word for the Holy Spirit, comes from the Greek *parakalein*. Dr. Barclay says that *parakalein* means exhorting troops who are about to go into battle. It is the word of the rallying call.[23] "FIGHT the good fight of faith." Pastoral love is love in conflict, love in the struggle, love on the battlefield. Truth-talk is war with words. Love in gear is creative conflict: the solving of conflict by talk. Communication with God changes your communication with people. Do you care enough to talk? Violence is the breakdown of communication by talk. If I do not love you I cut you off: I pay you my highest compliment if I care enough to hassle; in my words I make myself vulnerable to you. The Word become flesh (our Lord Jesus) communicates in words (the Bible) to teach us conflict-resolution through words (the Church). "In the beginning was the Word."[24] At the end, too, is the Word. Revelation 19:11 says, "Then I saw heaven open, and there was a white horse. Its rider is called Faithful and True.

. . . with justice he judges and fights his battles. His eyes were like a flame of fire, and he wore many crowns on his head. . . . The name by which he is called is 'The Word of God.' A sharp sword came out of his mouth. . . ." It is by the sharp sword coming out of his mouth that the Word of God defeats the nations, the organizations, the structures.[25] "As he is, so are we in the world."[26] Conflict in communication produces the new order. True love is tough love: without backbone it is mush. Only fighters can be leaders: love takes guts. "In this church," says a wise young pastor, "we encourage people to learn to fight. Fight and stay; fight, but don't leave; fight while we learn to love." Leadership demands conflict. "Who can defeat the world? Only he who believes that Jesus is the Son of God."[27] In love you learn the power of verbal combat.

Trusting God in Others

You cannot trust God in others unless you trust God in yourself. The greatest doubt is not questioning God's love; it is questioning God's love for you. Truth-think is the prerequisite for society reorganized. In the ultimate society we never lose sight of Christ's wounds: "The throne of God and of the Lamb shall be in it, and His servants shall worship Him . . . and they shall reign for ever and ever."[28] Servant-kings trust God in themselves so they can trust God in others. "Think of us as servants of Christ and managers who distribute God's hidden truth."[29] Paul's words describe you, the pastor. Your confidence in God's word comes from its power within you. Jesus said, "The Kingdom of God is like a man who scatters seed in his field. He sleeps at night, is up and about during the day, and all the while the seeds are sprouting and growing. Yet he does not know how it happens. *The soil itself makes the plants grow and bear fruit:* first the tender stalk appears, then the head, and finally the full head of grain."[30] In Greek the word is *automatos:* the seed of the Scripture keeps on growing in the soil of our hearts *automatically.* Your experience confirms Jesus' words. Delegating yourself to God, you delegate authority to people. *You trust the word of God within them.* You operate like your Lord: you trust God so you can trust others. "Through his faith we now have boldness and confidence. . . ."[31] You are a liberator: your control, your oppression, your tyranny change. You loose the people around you to be themselves.

Delegation

Delegation is self-denial. It is a positive act of trust. To trust God in others you deny yourself. The cross was Christ's self-denial, his trusting God not only for the resurrection but also for much more. He was trusting God for his organization. He was trusting God in us. His self-denial was the Church's self-affirmation. Without denying himself he could not affirm himself. And so it will be for you. Christ became nothing and received everything. The more I become nothing, the more I share his practical confidence. "He did not think equality with God something to be clutched or hoarded or grasped. . . . instead, of his own free will he gave it all up."[32] It is my "self" I give up. I exchange my life with Christ's: I become your servant. I cannot trust God in you without denying myself. Decentralization comes by delegation's self-denial: deliberate, conscious, positive acts of trust.

Decentralization

"Delegation" is when a man entrusts a woman with his sperm. "Decentralization" is when, together, they see their child grow up. Delegation is to decentralization what birth is to growth: what God begins, he completes. Delegation is man's free will; decentralization is Christ in you. Self-denial is neither periodic sacrifices nor dramatic heroics. It is a regular way you relate to other people. Delegation is God in creation: "God created man in his own image."[33] Decentralization is God in redemption: "If any man be in Christ he is a *new* creation."[34] In the cross, self-denial slaps you in the face. In creation, self-denial whispers in your ear. The God of crucifixion and the God of nature are one and the same God. Warren Hultgren says, "Nature is God's braille to a blind world."

Magnificent subtlety. God doesn't sign his initials in the corner of each sunset so we'll know who did it. He doesn't stamp his name like a laundry tag in the dew of each fresh field. There is no neon sign at the entrance of green forests, no tag line for credits on the panorama of the sea. Self-denial.

Remember the little girl whose father was a radio commentator? His work entranced her. At the family reunion she said their prayer of thanks. As the clan dutifully bowed in expectant reverence, her tiny voice piped up shattering the silence. Her soprano imitated Daddy's network bass: "This food comes to us courtesy of Almighty God!" Our Lord depends on his decentralized organizations. He denies himself. He doesn't do his own commercials.

Decentralization is slow work. Jesus did not trust himself to everyone. Neither will you. He trusted himself to "the men God has given him": the men who accepted his authority.[35] The only people who saw him after his resurrection were believers. Each of us has "the men God has given us." These people God calls us to lead and trust. For each of us the group is different. These are the people for whom you suffer. These are the people who need your self-denying love. Your trusting God in them will not be painless. Paul said to his flock in Colossae, "I rejoice in my sufferings for your sake. . . . I complete what is lacking in Christ's afflictions for the sake of his body, that is the Church. . . ."[36] To trust God in others costs you but saves them. When a daddy does not trust his children . . . what happens to them? Those children enact his fears. If I am scared that my children will become criminals, subconsciously I am driving them to crime. I expect them to be lawbreakers: they fulfill my expectations. "What the wicked dreads will come upon him."[37] The only way you can love your children is to trust God in them. They are "the men God has given you." Through you Christ decentralizes his body. As a positive act of trust you turn those under you loose.

Can Anybody Else Do It?

Am I my brother's keeper? No, I am my brother's brother; I am *not* my brother's Father. To let God be God is a big relief. I am *not* responsible for the world: only for my limited obedience as one small-sized human. In Christ I am freed from unreality too big for its britches. Finally now I am fitted to myself. Love comes only in human-sized packages. Every time I get bigger than human, love gets lost. Every son of God is also a son of man.

Willing to Let Go

How do you bring self-affirmation and self-denial together? You become realistic about your human limitations. You walk the path of your own obedience and no one else's. You are the *one and only* you. Self-affirmation—as you continue committing yourself—lets you know that God is in what you want. Self-denial—as you become willing to change your mind—makes you face, too, the desires of others. If God is in what I want to do, then (taking others as seriously as I take myself) I must consider whether or not God is in what others want me to do—even when their desires contradict my own. Self-denial—my submission—is one option. Authority—my resistance—is the other. Your relationships with other people demand that your relationship with God be continuous. Constantly you "let go and let God."

"Love your neighbor as yourself": what does the "B" Commandment mean?[38] Chaos, that's what it means, without Commandment "A"! Commandment "A" says you love God first. Loving God first makes Commandment "B" rational. Take the Good Samaritan, Jesus' famous hero from discrimination's minority race. The Good Samaritan bound up a broken traveler's wounds and cared for him after his roadside attack by theives. The priest and the Levite—superior religion—had passed the traveler by. The Good Samaritan was Jesus' answer to our question today: "Who is my neighbor?"

Recently I sat in a Bible discussion group studying the Good Samaritan. The leader asked for our reactions. Several members of the group expressed the guilt we share—we who skirt the road's other side to ignore the wounded traveler alongside our path. I agreed with them: who of us is innocent? Your neighbor is the person within your reach who needs your help. We are all bad neighbors. Then I shared with the group one other personal reaction of mine to the story. The Good Samaritan leaves me personally feeling relieved! Why? Social guilt. The widespread phenomenon of social guilt paralyzes us today. The Good Samaritan story tells me that I am *not* responsible for every traveler on every highway in the world. I may or may not be called into Highway Patrol work full time. I may or may not be called to organize Red Cross units for the Jericho Road. I may or may not be called to sociologic studies of highway gangs in greater Jerusalem's urban ghettos. My responsibility is to be a good neighbor in the when, where, and what I am. Accusations about the when, where, and what I am *not* do not come from the Jesus who told this story. The real guilt of Jesus' hearers was enough. He did not accuse them of responsibility for Palestine's crime wave, piling them with burdens too heavy for their overloaded backs. The story of the Good Samaritan teaches me responsible neighborliness, not sick self-destruction. It teaches appropriate service, not social suicide. It teaches me the call of a limited locale, the providence of personal proximity. C. G. Jung said you have no choice but to take the Devil inside yourself when you have no doctrine of Satan. The Good Samaritan helps us understand our Western age of anxiety. The Good Samaritan was one human covered with one particular highway's dust walking in the light of love, step by step. Social guilt is solved by personal obedience: Jesus' good neighbor did the good under his nose.

Are we, as social reformers, willing to let go of all our grandiose plans to remake the world . . . to let God change the world through others? Are we, as evangelicals, willing to let go of our tense, frantic evangelistic striving . . . to let God reach the world through others? The Christian life is always our learning to let go. You cannot make others responsible till you let go of your own prerogatives over them. God, the sovereign ruler of the world, the Responsible Executive, set out to make us into responsible executives too . . . by his own letting go. He "made himself of no reputation," His co-equality with his Father he "laid aside," he "made himself nothing," he "did not cling to his prerogatives as God's equal," he "emptied himself": HE LET GO.[39] Are we as preachers willing to let go of our pride in our own religious leadership . . . to let God change laymen through others? Are we, as laymen, willing to let go of our power over the clergy who serve us . . . to let God change preachers through others? Self-emptying—the kenotic Christ—made himself nothing. Zero leadership is leadership's infinity. Christ let go in order to take hold: the principle of the cross. Paul Tournier says it's like moving across life's circus on the trapeze. Before you take hold of your next swinging bar there comes a moment when you have to let go.

Building Up Others

You let go of yourself to build up others. If you believe in Christ you lead to love. Outside of Christ you love to lead. A Christian leader constantly asks, "Can anybody else do it?" You do only those jobs to which you are indispensable. The goal is a life of simplicity . . . Christ's quiet, calm, unhurried poise. In a General Motors research laboratory a sign hung high: "The Answer When Found Will Be Simple." Focus on Christ gives you eternity standing still in each leisurely moment. You have time to focus on other people. The Good Samaritan took time: the priest and the Levite were rushed. Maybe they were hurrying to a meeting on "How to Change the World"; I've stumbled over lots of people myself. God is in your interruptions. You can't build up others unless your pace is relaxed. The crucified life is not lived on the run: it's a walk, not a trot. Peter Drucker's *The Effective Executive* says that effective executives do not start with their tasks. They start with their time. Drucker advocates written time records for executives so they can find and eliminate their time waste. Only then can they develop a relaxed pace. He says your employees must feel "we have all the time in the world."

Delegation is self-love in behalf of others. "There has been for years a great deal of talk about 'delegation' in management," Drucker says. "Every manager, whatever the organization—business, government, university, or armed service—has been exhorted to be a better 'delegator.' I have yet to see any results. As usually presented, delegation makes little sense. If it means that somebody else ought to do part of 'my work' it is wrong. One is paid for doing one's own work. And if it implies the laziest manager is the best manager, it is not only nonsense: it is immoral. . . . But I have never seen an executive confronted with his time record who did not rapidly acquire the habit of pushing at other people everything that he need not do personally. Getting rid of anything that can be done by somebody else is a major improvement in effectiveness."[40] You get to your own job only by asking, "Can anybody else do it?" Those things which you, and no one else but you, can do, those things are God's will for you. You do the jobs to which you are indispensable. You start on this sequence of priorities: (1) your time with God; (2) your time with yourself; (3) your time with your family; (4) your time for your work. "Can anybody else do it?" keynotes your schedule. Is it your cup of tea? Does it have your name on it? Does it form the shape of your obedience? Not somebody else's, yours. Not, "Is it a good work?" But, "Is it a good work that is mine?" Can anybody else do it? means you accept your human limitations. Do you get battered by too many worthwhile demands for your time? Then you can do more by doing less. Thomas Kelly's classic *Testament of Devotion* says if you are centered in Christ you become as confident saying No as saying Yes.

You serve others by giving them responsibility. The leader's pattern is washing disciples' feet. The leader serves. His people walk their own road. He does not offer them crutches. He does not give them a chair. He does not carry them piggyback. He wants, not babies, but men. Leadership's badge is a basin and towel. The leader helps his men live step by step. He washes the dust away. Their steps will all be fresh. They walk on their own two feet. You let go and trust God in others. Jesus said, "He who believes in me will also do the works that I do; and greater works than these will he do, because I go to the Father."[41] Jesus returned to the Father so the Church might reach its full potential: a whole membership of responsible executives. He stepped back to build others up. God's kind of life—within himself—is Love decentralized. The Father honors the Son. The Spirit honors Christ. Christ honors the Father. Three in One: organization in God is a society of mutual support. You spotlight the other person. You push him forward. You help him grow great.

The Pastor Principle is responsibility passed on. Where you are indispensable you step forward. You assume command. Where you are not indispensable you step back. You build those under you up. You accept only that work to which you are essential in order to "serve one another in love." You make everyone around you important.[42] Everybody becomes a king. All the work is done by royalty. If ditch-digging is indispensable for me then I'm a ditch-digger. I step forward and assume command of my shovel. To servant-king ditch-diggers a shovel is a scepter. Every Indian becomes a chief. Good Samaritans let go in order to take hold. God loves the whole world: you just love your part. You do those tasks—only those tasks—nobody else can do: it is Love localized. Being a servant-king means your personal responsibilities are simplified.

Circumstances: God's Voice to You

God speaks to us in the language we know best—our circumstances.[43] This is the practical consequence of believing God is running the world—that someone who loves us is in charge. This fact—the sovereignty of God—underlay the rational assurance, the poised tranquillity of Jesus. Nothing happens to you—NOTHING—without the loving Father as its Engineer. When Evil's hand of blight strikes you, strikes those you love, strikes life surrounding you—your suffering calls you to the cross. With Jesus you say, "Why?" "Why me?" It is NOT wrong to say, "Why?" to God; it is human. If you knew "why," you wouldn't be you. When he said, "My God, my God, why hast thou forsaken me?" on the cross, Jesus identified with human sin and human limitation absolutely.[44] On the cross Jesus was indispensable—nobody else could do it. He cried out "Why?" for all mankind. God's *perfect* will—in a world of freedom and revolt—unfolds through his *permissive* will. He *permitted* Satan's revolt, mankind's fall, your suffering. His *perfect* will includes no revolt, no sin, no suffering. The cross—first for Jesus, then for us—is Moral Originality's way of getting God's *perfect* will accomplished. God's *perfect* will comes to us by means of his *permissive* will. The means and the end are one. Whatever happens to you, therefore, becomes part of the process. You "walk in the light." You recognize God's sovereign hand in your ordinary secular affairs. Oswald Chambers put it: "Nothing touches our lives but it is God Himself speaking. Do we discern His hand or only mere occurrence? Get into the habit of saying, 'Speak, Lord,' and life will become a romance. Every time circumstances press, say 'Speak, Lord'; make time to listen."[45] Doors open, doors close: God is speaking to you. Lights turn green to say "Go," lights turn red to say "Stop," lights turn yellow to say "Caution": through what happens in the developments around you God is speaking, telling you what to do.

Surrender to Sovereignty

"Luck" is an unchristian idea. "Lucky" and "unlucky" are superstition's sick way of thinking. The ideas of "good luck" and "bad luck" grapple with our human limitation and the Velvet Covered Brick—God's unshakable sovereignty. In Jesus Christ every man is lucky—unluckiness died at Calvary. Simplistic irrationalities like "lucky" or "unlucky" are inadequate for a sane view of life—they have robbed you of your will. Our sanity ultimately presupposes a sane God, alive, well, on the job, running everything. Satan operates only within God's permissive will. This God, who cannot be pushed over; this Leader, who is never shoved around; this Authority, who is unmovable gentleness—the Velvet Covered Brick—makes you like himself through your submission. You commit yourself to him in your nitty-gritty circumstances. Imaginary circumstances produce imaginary commitments; real situations bring you to commitments that are real. God's purpose is to make you like himself . . . in miniature. There are no short cuts. Satan's strategies always propose short cuts to good ends. "God educates us down to the scruple," says Chambers. "Christ continually submitted His spirit to God. I have the responsibility of keeping my spirit in continual agreement with His Spirit. Be serious with God and leave the rest gaily alone."[46] Heaven and hell: the means fit the ends. Complaining about your circumstances brings you hell on earth. Submitting to God—in your circumstances—turns earth into heaven. Jesus on the cross cried, "Why?" Was his "Why?" a complaint? Of course not. Just the opposite. It was Love's agony: a "why" of self-evaluation. "Why hast Thou forsaken me?" Tri-unity was paying the full price of Revolt's alienation. Following the "Why?" what did Jesus say? Immediately he said, "Father, into thy hands I *commit* my Spirit."[47] Self-evaluation by Jesus always turned into self-commitment. When you say, "Why?" to God in self-evaluation, God answers you as he knows best. Sometimes what he gives you is *not to know.* To be human is to question. But make one thing sure: your questioning must be followed by your commitment.

Optimistic Rocks

Can you imagine what a diamond goes through becoming a diamond? It starts out deep in the earth's bowels as a lump of coal. Endlessly it is burned. If carbon could talk, what would it say? "Stop, you're hurting me. Stop. Stop. I can't stand it!"

"But you're becoming a diamond!" you tell it. "The heat is refining you."

"I don't want to be a diamond! Leave me a lump of coal. It hurts too much! I can't stand this burning."

And you reply, "You stupid stone. You are receiving the highest compliment that could come to you. You will be mined and cut and polished. Your pain will exalt you. Soon you will become a solid piece of flashing fire." Whether the diamond can believe you or not doesn't change the fact. Jewels are only optimistic rocks.

Ours is an age of despair. Albert Camus says the only real question is whether or not to commit suicide. Our brightest people tell us life is absurd. Society without faith comes to the end of society: rebels growing old and pessimistic. "Enthusiasm" is life in God; from the Greek *en* ("in") plus *theos*, ("God"); in God you are enthusiastic. Your situation is never hopeless: crucifixions precede resurrections. In 1953 drama critic George Jean Nathan caught our mood: "An optimist is the kind of person who believes a housefly is looking for a way to get out."[48] Is that Christian optimism? Absolutely not. Naïve optimism is never Christian. Christian optimism is cynical optimism. If you are cynical about yourself (in me dwells no good thing; Christ is my righteousness), then you have a healthy cynicism about others. It keeps you from misplaced trust. Imagining a housefly wanting out is misplaced trust in the fly. So you either (1) figure the fly may stay awhile and adjust to his company, or (2) find a fly swatter. Christian optimism counts on either (1) an external change in your situation, or (2) an internal change in your attitude.

This kind of optimism dances up even when you're down. However bad things get, you are in the process of being fashioned into Christlikeness. Romans 8:28 is one of the Bible's mountain peaks: "All things work together for good to those who love God, to those who are called according to his purpose . . . to be conformed to the image of his Son." In all your everydayness, God is at work like a craftsman on a prize-winning exhibit, like an artist on a consummate masterpiece. "We are God's workmanship," says Ephesians 2:10, his handicraft. The Greek word is *poiema*, translated "poem": you are God's poetry; all the lines are getting polished.

Optimism about your own circumstances gives you optimism about others. Christian optimism is organizationally contagious. The leader sets the tone. Jesus gave each of us who believe, another "Comforter," "Advocate," "Helper," "Encourager" like himself. In Jewish courtrooms the "Paraclete," *the advocate,* stood over against the "Kategoros," *the accuser.*[49] The Spirit of Satan withers, condemns, accuses. The Spirit of God boosts, encourages, affirms. In Christ every man has undreamed-of potential. Optimism is a realistic assessment of every person you lead. Eternal life makes you patient. God built every man to be a servant-king. Discouragement is of the Devil. Whatever your circumstances, "let your hope keep you joyful."[50] Tradition's view of the Christian life means deliverance *from* trouble. It is wrong. Eternity's view of the Christian life means deliverance *in* trouble. Completely different. Christ in you has already whipped your situation.

Ruled by the Spirit's Peace

Suffering is the hallmark of Christian leadership that is genuine. "God had only one son without sin but He never had one without suffering," said St. Augustine. It is never easy to love a rebel. Authentic leadership hurts. You lean into your pain. You identify yourself with Christ's cross . . . with the one relationship that is essential. You concentrate continually on your own relationship with Christ himself. Other people become shadows. But what is the effect? You see other people with Christ's eyes! Knowing Christ gives you understanding of others—heightened—even while you concentrate on them less. The Christ you focus on made them too. Your suffering becomes increasingly intelligent. Progressively you become freed from suffering that is sick. No healthy person *wants* to suffer. Psychologists call the sick desire to suffer "masochism." The word "masochism" came from Leopold von Sacher-Masoch, a nineteenth-century Austrian writer, just as "sadism," the sick desire to inflict suffering on others, came from the Marquis Donatien de Sade: both "sadism" and "masochism" fight against creative, therapeutic, Christian suffering.

How do you discriminate? How do you tell the difference? The answer brings us to the heart of Christianity. Of course you use all the resources we have outlined: the Bible, the Christian group, the structure, self-love and self-denial, a relaxed schedule, the practical developments as God's voice to you. But are these enough? From the Bible to circumstances these are *external* voices. Is there anything *internal* to corroborate the way you read them? Of course there is. *The peace of the Holy Spirit in your heart. God guides you by his peace. Your intellect is joined by your emotions. His name is "the God of Peace."*[51]

The Christian life is normal, natural, relaxed humanity: man as he was intended. The legalist says, "Everything's wrong unless it's right"; the Christian says, "Everything's right unless it's wrong." Both Creation (God made everything) and Incarnation (God lived in what he made) tell you why your simple physical needs strike you—without your even thinking about them—as right. You breathe air, you drink water, you go to sleep, you wake up, on and on and on. About these basic natural processes you are at peace. You eat because eating *feels* right. You know how good, calm, and comfortable eating *feels* long before you can explain rationally about nutrition and nourishment and calories. Your *feeling of peace* has been God's way to guide you into regular eating. Now go a step higher. Why do you brush your teeth? This is more complicated. Tooth decay is something about which you have *learned.* It is tied to the emotional instinct of self-preservation. Brushing your dental enamel, preserving your molars, protecting your smile, is a practice you have been taught. Self-love translated into a hygiene habit makes it feel right. God's peace guides you to brush your teeth. Take the principle now to its highest application. Christian obedience illuminates your education with all the wisdom of biblical insight. Then it applies the peace of God to everything you do. "Let the peace of God rule in your hearts."[52] God speaks deep within you and tells you what to do by his inward peace. You make your choices by calmness.

If There's a Doubt, Don't

Life is mostly fun. Look at the infinite choices we face in living, and you realize that God hasn't given us many "no-no's." The more you learn of him and the more you learn of yourself, the more you understand that every one of the commandments— every "no-no"—is for your own good. They weren't given to ruin our happiness, but to make our happiness practical and possible. In my next book (on authority and submission, sex, and the family) I hope to illustrate this controversial fact more thoroughly. But any organization can teach it to you. Recently an executive in one of our Foundations was furious with me. A third employee—who works under him as well as under me—has been giving us both lots of static. This third person wants to quit. I hoped he would stay. I tried to get him to change his mind. I failed. His immediate superior felt our suffering was unnecessary. "Let the man quit," he moaned. I cannot explain why I felt no inner liberty, no peace of mind, no calmness of soul about terminating our conversations with this upset friend who wanted to leave us. Intuitively I knew I had no choice. All I could do was talk a little—and pray a lot. The ruckus persisted for months! Finally last week our answer came clear. A fourth person, whom none of us had been considering at all, entered the dialogue. Almost overnight our answers have emerged to the benefit of the whole organization. The resigning employee will leave, but his departure will be infinitely more constructive than if he had gone prematurely.

How do I get my signals as a Christian leader? "Have no anxiety, but in everything make your requests known to God in prayer with thanksgiving. Then the peace of God, which is beyond our utmost understanding [of far more worth than human reasoning], will keep guard over your hearts and your thoughts, in Christ Jesus."[53] If there's a doubt, don't. If you're not sure, wait. "In your patience possess ye your souls."[54] Conflict with my executive associate was painful. It shook me because he is a man of God. George Macdonald's insight helped: If a thing strikes you as darkness, label it darkness regardless of who says it is light. It would be better that you stand rebuked before the judgment bar of God than that you call light what strikes you as darkness.[55] Satan counterfeits many of God's gifts. He cannot counterfeit our inward peace. That deepest, calmest, sweetest, surest sense of inner calm—that is God's hand of assurance to you. Do not move without it. The prickly uneasiness in your guts, the jangling driving compulsion, the inward electric agitation—these warn you about spirits that are alien. Never violate God's peace. The final arbiter, the court of last resort, your surest guide, is calmness. Jesus said, "Peace I leave with you; my peace I give to you; not as the world gives do I give to you. Let not your hearts be troubled, neither let them be afraid."[56] The Revised Standard Version calls the Holy Spirit our "Counselor." He is the "Lord of peace." The Kingdom of God within you is joy and peace.[57] Robert Raines says you "listen to your insides." You act only on your good vibrations. You don't make any move unless deep inside you it feels right, good, and comfortable. A soft, quiet, calm, gentle glow turns on inside your stomach.

Relaxed, Calm, Confident Timing

Pastoral Authority grows out of the assurance that God can, will, and does guide people personally and individually. The entire Bible, from Abraham in Ur of the Chaldees to St. John on the Isle of Patmos, rests on this conviction. If you doubt God's personal guidance in your own everyday affairs, you really doubt the whole ball of wax. Obedience to the Holy Spirit makes you unpredictable, spontaneous, creative. You become faithful, fearless, courageous, not by rules but by a relationship. Sometimes you express Christ's nature of Authority. Sometimes his nature of Submission. Christ over and within you tells you which and when.

In tennis it's your timing that counts. If I hit my forehand late I sacrifice power. The racquet face falls open so the ball flies off to the right. If I hit the ball early I sacrifice power too. The racquet face gets closed so the ball flies off to the left. Perfect power means perfect timing. Crucifixion is submission; resurrection is authority: the Kingdom of God is the Kingdom of Restraint; the Kingdom of Gratification Deferred; the Kingdom of Perfect Timing. This morning I played tennis here at our home. As I played I thought about how the Holy Spirit works within us. The Bible's symbolism pictures the Holy Spirit as a dove. While I played I heard the beautiful call floating across the foliage around our court of one of our Texas doves. Not the raucous jabbering of a mocker or the staccato percussion of a woodpecker—the dove's call is soft, gentle, soothing, the undulating whirr of quiet music. I thought how the stillness of God's voice within us, the quiet music of our inmost souls, depends on his sovereign timing. Many Christians are discouraged today about the Church. They are in despair about our age. Quit worrying. God's timing is never off. His method is always a man. He is at work now within you. I got my reassurance today reading Professor Hollander's study of secular leadership. "The absence of influence-acceptance in the face of an assertion of influence does not necessarily mean that the influence agent is powerless. It could mean that he does not fully assert the influence potential at his command. This matter of restraint in the use of power available in imposed organizational structures is a necessarily vital condition for smooth relationships. Where the person in authority consistently uses the full power of his position, he undercuts his long-term effectiveness."[58] Pastoral Authority is power long-term. Timing is the key and no man holds it: it rests in the Father's hand.

> ". . . Still with unhurrying chase,
> And unperturbed pace,
> Deliberate speed, majestic instancy . . ."[59]
> Eternity explodes in time.
> Each pregnant second celebrates
> The triumph of the sovereign Servant-King.

We have listed seven keys to experiencing God's guidance, knowing his will, when to assert and when to submit. Let me summarize them by listing again the topic headings, along with seven synonyms beginning with "S" to make them easier for you to remember. The "Seven S's of Pastoral Authority":

(1) The Word of Authority: *Scripture*
(2) Your Duty of Enjoyment: *Self-love*
(3) Who's in Charge Here? *Structure*
(4) Trusting God in Others: *Self-denial*
(5) Can Anybody Else Do It? *Simplification*
(6) Circumstances: God's Voice to You: *Situations*
(7) Ruled by the Spirit's Peace: *Serenity*

You can recognize what God is telling you to do, everyday.

VIII

The Church Principle
for Every Organization

Honor Christ by submitting to each other.
Ephesians 5:21

The Church is not buildings; the Church is people. I'm in Church everywhere I go. I'm in Church as I sit here writing in the garden patio outside the bedroom wing of our house. Two tiny lizards are climbing the Arkansas ledgestone walls before my eyes, flipping their skin-shaped color charts. To nature's Author, for such a fascinating display, I give my thanks. Life gives you an infinite variety of services for worship. Here in the garden I am part of the Church dispersed. Sunday morning with our Parkdale congregation I am part of the church gathered. In both places I am in Church. The New Testament doesn't talk about being a member of the Church; it talks about being a member of Christ. I have no life apart from Christ's body: I am a member (an organ, an outreach) of Christ; he in me, I in him. I'm in Church all the time.

Our work in group life out of Laity Lodge has taught me a very basic lesson. Walking in the light is always and only the experience of the group. "Fellowship one with another" is the stamp of Christian authenticity . . . lonely Christianity is a fraud. The Pastor Principle is a picture of creative organizational authority. The Church Principle is a picture of creative organizational participation. Group life demands unity between the leader and the led. Submission enables a group to love its leader. Constructive conflict requires every person to be a pastor; the Church under Christ organizes equals: voluntary submission is love. The Pastor Principle is loving leadership. The Church Principle is loving membership.

Remember the Church Principle from Chapter 4: *"Organiza-tions demand followers. Followers lead by serving their leaders. They lead by serving; in serving they lead. Under the Spirit of the Father and the Son. Amen."*

Can you love people up the Establishment ladder ahead of you? This ability was Christ and his apostles' moral genius: agile *agape.* Because they, too, saw themselves as leaders, they loved tyrants on top of them in their social, political, and religious organizations. To love those below you is not so difficult. Both Jesus' conflict with Judas and Paul's fight with the Judaizers teach you why. Both Judas and the Judaizers showed great concern for people who were poor.[1] The explanation for their attitudes is simple. You can love those below you without affecting your pride. Your posture is superior condescension, magnanimous moral conceit. But to love the man above you is different. To love him without flattery or self-abasement, to love him without bitterness or resentment, to love him in the midst of conflict and pain: to love the man above you is love's highest hurdle—you cannot get over it alone. You cannot do it without the cross inside lifting you up. You cannot do it without resurrection power so you can step down. Loving the leader on top is essential to social peace. Organizational love— "submitting yourselves to one another in the fear of God"—is peace made rational. No other formula unravels our inmost inter-personal snarls. In submission's warm power tangles between us evaporate. Have you learned how to yield?

In February 1962 the University of Chicago conducted a semi-nar on "The Creative Organization." Under Dean George P. Shultz of the School of Business—now Secretary of the Treasury in Washington—Graduate Professor Gary Steiner coordinated the meeting. For three days, 16 scientists, scholars, and executives talked: Franz Alexander, chief of psychiatry at Los Angeles' Mount Sinai Hospital; B. E. Benswinger, chief executive of the Brunswick Corporation; management consultant Marvin Bower of McKinsey and Company; Harvard's Jerome Bruner of the Cen-ter for Cognitive Studies; David Ogilvy of Ogilvy, Benson and Mather Advertising; Peter Peterson, president of Bell and Howell; along with the distinguished others. At the end Professor Steiner summarized. In the conference book he edited, distilled from these discussions, he outlined six traits of "the creative organization." I modify one slightly and add another, passing them on to you as the basic skeleton for my own summarizing conclusion. Not surprisingly (and yet uncannily too) they describe the authentic Church. You see the Church Principle all around you everywhere.

A Sense of Who You Are

Professor Steiner says: "The Creative Organization is different . . . and knows it. It is not trying to be like others."[2] Organizational identity comes from identity that is individual. Billy Graham says every man is born an original and dies a copy. That risk for me, ironically, involved Billy himself. Billy has been a father-figure to me. His encouragement has helped me incalculably. But at Laity Lodge I began developing a style of program different from Billy's. In the Layman's Leadership Institutes I tied both strands together —the proclamation emphasis from crusades combined with the participation emphasis from small groups. At one stage I found myself worrying lest Billy be displeased. Is any one of you, besides me, a worrier? Pharisees Anonymous for me turns out to be Anonymous Anxiety. I worry about myself, I worry about the country, I worry about the business, I worry about my family, I worry about what others think. Then I go to church and hear that worry is a sin! So I worry about that, too!

But somewhere along the line I remember that God *loves* worriers. I remember that Christ died to give me victory over my fears. I truth-think. I thank God my worries got conquered at Calvary! I relax, receiving Christ as my peace.[3] It makes all the difference—because it allows me to *be* different. With Billy Graham it allows me to be myself. Fathers and sons are each unique. Freedom from slavery to each other is why Jesus said, "Call no man father on earth."[4] And of course, as you would expect, I have found that Billy's love for me is not conditioned on my being like him—working in a pattern that is distinctively his. He affirms my freedom to be different, willing to let me go free. Love always lets you be yourself. The 13th chapter of I Corinthians, on love, is preceded by the 12th chapter, on differences. "Christ is like a single body with its many limbs and organs . . . a body is not one single organ, but many. Suppose the foot should say 'Because I am not a hand, I do not belong to the body.' . . . Suppose the ear were to say 'Because I am not an eye I do not belong to the body.' If the body were all ear, how could it smell? But, in fact, God appointed each limb and organ to its own place in the body, as he chose. If the whole were one single organ, there would not be a body at all. . . . God has combined the various parts of the body . . . so there might be no sense of division in the body, but that all its organs might feel the same concern for each other. If one organ suffers, they all suffer together. If one flourishes, they all rejoice together: You are Christ's body now, and each of you a limb or organ of it." In Christ you are unrepeatably the one and only you.

Cowards and Conflict

Relationships without stress are relationships unreal. To accept reality in relationships is to accept our tensions. In Christ conflict forces our relationships to grow. For years I ran from conflict. As a boy I hated a fight—probably because I was physically little. I sit here now running my tongue over the chipped corner of one of my front teeth. It reminds me of a junior high fight on a school playground more than thirty years ago. Miller Overall hit me and broke that tooth. I turned and walked away. Why didn't I tie into him? Was he too big? No, I was too scared! Other fights I won: by the water fountain at Camp Stewart's gymnasium I got a bully down; by the ebony tree next to the driveway in our Harlingen front yard one battle was mine; I savor again the sweet taste of triumph. But Miller Overall and my chipped front tooth remind me of fights when I ran away. A singsong taunt from my grade school playground comes back to me now: "Howard, Coward, Buttermilk Soured!" Over and over and over again.

"The cowards, the traitors, and the perverts," said St. John, "the place for them is the lake burning with fire . . . which is the second death."[5] "Lord Jesus, forgive me for fleeing my fight with

Miller Overall. Thank you that you do. Christ is my strength. Christ is in me now. Amen." Christ in you is courage. Today—grown up—Miller Overall and I could talk.

Each Unique and Different

Your individuality cannot come without conflict. Other people under or above you will not be able to find their individuality without conflict, either. Don't let the conflict scare you. "In the world you shall have tribulation."[6] Discouragement about America's generation gap fails to see its potential. Jesus said, "I came not to bring peace but a sword."[7] What did he mean? He meant that all of us—parents and children alike—are rebels, rebellious anarchists underneath, rebellious tyrants on top. God is in the tension. Slavery to Christ himself is our only freedom. Authority-and-Submission gives you a way to think about conflict that is positive. Often what we call rebellion is not rebellion at all; it is a healthy assertion of oncoming leadership. How much "adolescent revolt" is really a teenager's emerging assertion of his adult authority? And God-given! We parents see it as revolt only because our own rebellion—against our earthly parents, against our Heavenly Parent—is projected onto our children. Rebels-on-top-tyrants cannot let their children go free. Think Authority-and-Submission about your conflicts and you think positive. Negative thinking locks you into a cycle of revolutionary despair. Mao Tse-tung argues for continual revolution—killing millions regularly—because he has no way to think that is positive. Poor man . . . poor people. Christ in you is "Yea and Amen" . . . the riches of thinking affirmatively.[8] Norman Vincent Peale in *The Power of Positive Thinking* thought straight. Conflict—if you learn to think positive—is your individuality heightened.

Independent Yet United

"The Creative Organization is independent" . . . indigenous, autonomous.[9] Church organization is irrepressibly free. It is modeled on the Trinity . . . hierarchy combined with equality . . . independence combined with unity. Deity decentralized gives you decentralized organizations. The Trinity is the One God, decentralized. This Heavenly Ideal within you here on earth teaches you never to let yourself be surprised by controversy. It's the centralization-decentralization conflict. "If they hated me they will also hate you . . . friendship with the world is enmity with God."[10] *Fear of conflict hamstrings any leader.* Love gets angry: "Be angry and sin not."[11] God commands you to get angry. Only in Jesus Christ can you get angry and not sin. When your authority is challenged and you do not fight back you do not care about yourself, neither do you care about the person who has violated your integrity. True love is tough love. As a brick sits steady, love fights back. Between God the Father and God the Son there is no conflict: perfect centralization perfectly decentralized. The new style in human organization arrived in Christ Jesus: perfect command in the Father, perfect obedience in the Son. "I and the Father are One": perfect obedience in perfect command.[12] Nobody else on earth—either in command or in obedience—is perfect, so now you face inevitable conflict. The closer you and your associates get to Christlikeness—perfection in command and perfection in obedience—the less you have organizational conflict, the more you have organizational peace. The Church in the world is love in gear—conflict that is creative—truth-talk where people care about you.

Submission Is a Two-Way Street

Fear of conflict hamstrings any follower. Christians bring independence and unity together only through two-way submission. Organizationally, submission flows from the bottom up: I submit to my boss above me; my wife submits to me above her; citizens submit to the ruling government; laymen submit to pastors above them. But—if the man on top knows he is a sinner and wants to change—submission also flows from the top down. My wife, my children, my group, and my employees become God's appointed ministers to help me change. I encourage my children to see themselves as my pastors. Lord Chesterfield said, "Children and subjects are much seldomer in the wrong than parents and kings." "Always mistrust a subordinate who never finds fault with a superior," said Collina. If a parent wants to change from a sinner into a saint, he welcomes his children's help. He creates a climate of openness around himself. His children become free to speak their deepest feelings out. Our children's free thoughts contain both truth and error: they speak to us for God and Satan both. If you are seeking God as a parent, you will sense when your child is speaking the truth to you. Your child is your equal: he can be your pastor. The Church Principle releases two-way love between parents and children. You unlock the power of submission from the top down:

(1) The power of children to change their parents.

(2) The power of employees to change their bosses.

(3) The power of laymen to change their pastors.

I learn from my children. They help me grow up. "Wilt thou be made whole?" Do you want to get well? "Be perfect, as your Father in heaven is perfect." Do you want to change?[13] "To say, 'Oh, I'm no saint,' is acceptable to human pride, but it is unconscious blasphemy against God. It literally means that you defy God to make you into a saint, 'I am much too weak and hopeless, I am outside the reach of the Atonement.' "[14] God speaks through those you lead. "Remember that to change thy mind and follow him that sets thee right, is to be none the less the free agent that thou wast before," said Marcus Aurelius. When you live a life of two-way submission, truth springs up around your feet. You submit to the people under you and you come into your glory.

To Submit Is to Suffer

Because every leader—as well as every follower—is a rebel, submission inevitably means suffering. To be a Christian is to suffer. Today between Barbara Dan and me a big argument boiled over. This coming weekend I want us together to fly to Dallas. She does not want to go. I think the trip is for her welfare as well as mine.

I admit it—I may be wrong—it's a long story. I am not only a fallible man, fallibility with me is a disease. But I cannot get any inner calm about spending this weekend at home. I have no choice but to insist on the trip. In our house today I see my wife's pain. *She knows: to submit is to suffer.* Is Barbara Dan the rebel or am I? We cannot be sure. God is our judge. Neither of us has to be right. But with schedules to be rearranged, children to be cared for, and complications in the household, my wife is hurting. Naturally I hurt too. Conflict with your wife hurts bad. I could rationalize the situation and back down—but could I, really? I want to be submissive to God—to be a velvet-covered brick, not a brick-headed tyrant. *I know too: to submit is to suffer.* Of the two of us, her pain is greater. To submit to God is easier than to submit to people. Yet already I sense Barbara Dan is adjusting. She respects the structure. Between the two of us today, the step she has taken as a Christian is bigger than mine. Your submission to God stands inseparable from your submission to people. My wife's power with me now is greater than ever. Her love—expressed to me in submission—has made my love for her grow. By "losing" she has "won." She is more herself; I am more myself: together we make more of a unit.

Wanting to Work Hard

"The Creative Organization works hard." Healthy relationships turn loose within us rivers of psychic energy. You work hard because you want to. You are drawn, not driven. You "work out your own salvation": what God works IN you work OUT.[15] Christ in his Church—a society of Submission—unites you with the Energy that creates and sustains everything: "Work is love made visible."[16] Love made visible is work.

Saints and Their Sweat

Jesus worked: labor has never been the same. When the Voice from heaven said, "This is My beloved Son in whom I am well pleased," he had never been anything but a carpenter.[17] The excellence of his carpentry revealed God's integrity. "No crooked table leg or ill-fitting drawer ever, I dare swear, came out of the carpenter's shop of Nazareth," said Dorothy Sayers. "Nor if they had could anyone have believed they were made by the same hand that made heaven and earth."[18] Shoddy workmanship in America —your television repair; your automobile breakdown; your grocer's service; your washer, your dryer, your lawnmower on the blink— shoddy work calls for the ordinary believer's priesthood. Nevil Shute wrote *Round the Bend* about men who made a new religion from the excellence of their work. They needn't have. Real Christianity wears work clothes. Every believer is a worker-priest. Excellence is in God's heart. Shabby work says we have not got there yet. Don Williams, one of the West Coast's Street Christians' leaders, told me about a poster at one of their rallies: "After Jesus Everything Else Is Toothpaste!" I riotously agree. One taste of Reality spoils you for anything else. And the other side is that Jesus is in toothpaste, too. If God chose a burning bush to show the sanctity of daily work, he most certainly is with you at your lavatory. You get rid of cavities, not by supernatural spectacular inexplicable mystical magical dentistry, but by brushing your teeth. The pious preacher stood by his farmer-deacon looking out across green rows of head-high corn. "Brother Jones," the parson said, "the Lord and you sure have done a fine job with this farm." The deacon rubbed his toe in the dirt. "Ah reckon we have, preacher," he said, "but you should 'a seen it when the Lord had it by hisself." *Presumption* is not faith. You don't get good farms without hard-working farmers. "Whatever you do, work at it with all your heart, as though you were working for the Lord, and not for men."[19]

Being Is Believing Is Doing

Christ *syncopates* work: the Sabbath Commandment means your rest and your work are in rhythm. "God blessed the seventh day and hallowed it, because on it God rested from all his work."[20]

Do you syncopate your work and your rest? How many depressions, heart attacks, ulcers, breakdowns are really sabbaths overdue? "Sabbath" means rest. Keeping the sabbath means more than staying home from work or going off to church. Keeping the letter you can miss the law's spirit. I'm a living testimony: Wayne Oates says religious people temperamentally become "workaholics."[21] Christ in you is sabbath rest. Your life begins to look like music: you move in flowing balance. The secret of your rhythm is found in Matthew's Gospel: "Come unto me, all you who are weary and heavy laden and I will give you rest."[22] Come to Christ and rest. Not lazy rest, though: working rest. "Take my yoke upon you and learn of me." Yoke means work. Christ is activity: in him you work. But while you work you rest. "And you shall find rest for your souls." And while you rest you work. "For my yoke is easy and my burden is light." Christ is rest surrounded by work and work surrounded by rest. Your life tunes in. To a man suffering from his exhaustion, given out in overwork, Christ never means effort. To a man suffering from lack of purpose, paralyzed by his boredom, Christ never means laziness. What your schedule needs at this everlasting moment, Christ is. In the days of his flesh our Lord showed us a perfect schedule: eternity wrapped up in time. St. John tells us the robe he wore was seamless.[23] In him too, your time becomes continuous. Working or resting you constantly come to him. Your schedule, like his, woven from top to bottom, becomes a solid tapestry without a seam. The old Yiddish proverb says, "Sleep faster. We need the pillows." But you can't rush rest. "He who believes will not be in haste."[24] The dormancy of winter precedes the energy of spring. Don't try to repeal the season. Rest each day, each week, each season, each year—to catch step with life's cadence we work when we work, play when we play, rest when we rest, in balanced alternated sequence. Syncopation is flexibility. Routine is a part of rest; regularity helps you relax, but to worship your routine or idolize your regularity means you picked the wrong God. Christ's syncopated work or else your own jumbled-up exhaustion: these are your alternatives. Orderly work and disciplined relaxation, in rhythm, or else creative juices so thinned out they're too pooped to percolate. Christ puts his inner harmony into me: music in my soul. Work begins to look like dancing. My tedium is broken by a blast of joyous jazz.

He works through you. The Church Principle is BEING at work; BELIEVING is DOING: faith is sanctified sweat. David Ogilvy told the conference on Creative Organization, "Great work in art has almost never been created by rich artists who were free to play around. It has been created by poor artists who had to create something very good . . . to eat. Handel wrote *The Messiah* because he was broke."[25] Christ means you work. But you also rest. Jerome Bruner of Harvard told the conference the other side, "I never visited a lab that was any good where the people weren't having a lot of fun."[26]

My pastor, with a fellow group of ministerial students, once worked in a J. C. Penney stockroom. The manager was profane, but he knew good work. One weekend the preachers heard his comment to his assistant manager: "Those damn Christians *work harder* than anybody in this store."

Fact-Founded Decisions

"The Creative Organization," says Professor Steiner's conference summary, "separates sources from information; that is, it has an objective, fact-founded approach. . . . It is able to draw on facts wherever it can find them and evaluate them in their own right, rather than depending blindly upon the authorities in the field."[27] Submitting to God you "separate source from information." True information all comes from the God who IS Truth. I am freed from any and all of my human sources. Christ frees me from being anybody's "yes man." "No men" give you revolution; "yes men" give you tyranny; "fact men" give you freedom. "Howard," you say, "can you really believe the Church Principle heightens your understanding of facts? Didn't the church suppress Galileo? Didn't Darwin have to fight the church? Didn't the clergy oppose Copernicus?" You misunderstand the Church Principle. The institutional church—Protestant, Catholic, Orthodox, What-not— is mixed. Fallible and infallible, bad and good, false and true. You don't put your eyes on the fallible church. You put your eyes on the infallible Christ. "Looking to Jesus the pioneer and perfecter of our faith."[28] The fact of Christ's death and resurrection illuminates the world of facts. Truth-think is the reason ignorance, prejudice, and superstition have had their day. In Jesus Christ our Lord we have entered the age of facts.

True Humanity and Truth-Talk

The *Times Literary Supplement* (London) called Herbert Butterfield's (1949) *Christianity and History* "the most outstanding pronouncement on the meaning of history since Acton's [1895] Inaugural": Butterfield said, "Each of us should do the good that is straight under our noses. Those people work more wisely who seek to achieve good in their own small corner of the world and then leave the leaven to leaven the whole lump, than those who are forever thinking that life is vain unless one can act through the central government, carry legislation, achieve political power, and do big things."[29] William Blake put it, "he who would do good to another must do it in minute particulars."[30] Christianity's "minute particulars" may be unstylish, but they are the only way to change the world. "Genius is the capacity for infinite attention to detail," said Carlyle.[31] Moral creativity in personal relationships —love's patient spontaneity—may be undramatic, but it alone is ultimately practical. Dag Hammarskjöld said, ". . . without the humility and warmth which you have to develop in your relations to the few with whom you are personally involved, you will never be able to do anything for the many."[32] From a Secretary-General's perspective in the United Nations, he spoke quite a mouthful. Mass morality turns out immoral. To think big you learn to think little. Jesus concentrated on the twelve men around him, and, out from there, on their relationships. All our vast expanses of utopian social planning, all our joint transcontinental evangelistic blitzkriegs, all our solutions overnight, of every good sort—run jolt into this incontrovertible fact: Jesus concentrated primarily on the twelve.

Church Authority and Truth-Think

Swiss therapist Paul Tournier tells us about Bishop Wurm, one of
the leaders in the Confessing Church, heroically standing up to
Hitler in Nazi Germany. How hard it was, Bishop Wurm told Dr.
Tournier, at the beginning of Hitler's reign, to know what attitude
the church should take toward this tremendous popular movement, whipping up the masses.

> Should the church step in line, in spite of the movement's obvious
> flaws, in the hope of influencing the regime and of directing it
> toward a true national renewal? Or must the church fight the Nazi
> regime, thus losing all contact with the masses? True, the new
> leaders committed grave injustices, and professed doctrines quite
> contrary to the Christian faith. But was this not the case of most
> political leaders, at least to some degree? Resist or surrender: which
> should they do? Bishop Wurm discussed this often with a close
> friend, a fellow bishop, who was equally hesitant. Then one night
> Bishop Wurm suddenly felt called by God to break with the
> regime. He obeyed the divine call. Happily so, for he was but a hair
> breadth from becoming inextricably involved, through compro-
> mise upon compromise, to the point where he never could have
> stopped. Thus these two close friends, having long hesitated to-
> gether, became the leaders of the two factions in the church which
> became irreconcilably opposed to each other.[33]

Bishop Wurm's submission to God gave him power. In Hitler's
Nazi Germany he asserted his pastoral authority . . . in fact.

During the war a young German theologian, Dr. Eberhard
Müller, served as a chaplain on the Russian steppes. He began to
dream about the days to come, after the time the Third Reich's
mad catastrophe had blazed to its inevitable end. What could he
do to straighten out the disorder in so many minds? He began to
dream of training centers for jurists, doctors, teachers, merchants,
housewives, politicians, technicians, artists, peasants; training centers for laymen. So, toward the end of the war, Dr. Müller described his dreams to Bishop Wurm. With support from the
bishop, he founded the first Evangelical Academy. Dr. Tournier
reports, "I took part in the first medical session, in May 1946.

That experience had a great influence upon my life. For ten years I had felt called to concentrate my study upon the role of the spiritual life in the health of men. But up until this time I had been very much alone. Then [at this first training session for physicians] I discovered that the most learned medical men were very much concerned with this same relationship, even those who up until then had had virtually no contact with the church."[34] Today, as I write, I share Dr. Tournier's sense of indebtedness. In 1959, struggling to give birth to Laity Lodge in Texas half a world away from Germany, Leonard Holloway and I traveled to Europe and visited the Lay Academies. Bishop Wurm's pastoral authority proved contagious worldwide. Equality combined with hierarchy gives you a creative church of contagious authority.

Crazy Ideas and Sane Encouragement

"The Creative Organization," says Professor Steiner's summation, "has more irrational impulses within it, and on the other hand, more effective controls for keeping these impulses in the appropriate channels."[35] The Church believes that Jesus Christ's IDEAS are essential for human sanity. Obviously this fact neither keeps it from exposing broadside all its lunatic fringes, nor enables any of us in it to claim that we are 100 percent. In his last years Paul wrote, "I do not consider myself to have 'arrived' "; today *our* troubles come when *we think we have.*[36] It is precisely this knowledge—that none of us has arrived—which gives the Church its safeguards. All us humans have problems . . . the question is whether or not we admit it.

> You are right, Mr. Chamberlayne,
> You are no case for my sanatorium:
> You are much too ill.[37]

T. S. Eliot says it for us: the sickest man of all is the man who cannot admit he is sick. The Church shows up your craziness (and mine) just like a magnifying glass. Christians keep on keeping-on, submitting their sicknesses to Jesus Christ's health. The Church is a long-term hospital.

The language of revolution is not the language of the Bible.

Both Jesus and modern psychiatry agree that our words reveal our inmost selves. The language of Idealized Revolution reveals how far we find ourselves today from God's kind of thinking. To dramatize our cause you can hear both conservatives and liberals—alike—talking about "Christian Revolution." Mish-mash. There is no such thing. Christianity is God's order. At issue is not simply that we are verbally imprecise. Christians must be able to see every structure, every institution, every organization from the viewpoint of both the leader and the led. Christians must be able to see their own lives, individually, socially, churchwide, as lives of orderly discipline. Christ did not talk about revolutionary upheaval; he talked about his disciples' obedience. He did not speak of the grasp for earthly power; he spoke of therapeutic suffering. The New Order is order. The Kingdom of God is kingdom. The Family of God is family. "Christian Revolution" is gibberish upside down. The language of the Bible is the language of Christian submission. The formula for society made new is Submissive Authority. We are out to get rid of the tyranny of irrational thoughts.

Tomorrow's Thinking Today

Human psychology is the psychology of pride and revolution. Adler described our struggle: "from below to above"; we cannot fulfill ourselves—we fall, unable to transcend. Jesus says, "He that saves his life shall lose it." You get on top and find out you're still below. *Divine psychology* is the psychology of humility and submission. The Servant-King as a gift: "from above to below"; now he bids us come and die—in him we share transcendence. "He that loses his life for my sake shall find it," said Jesus.[38] God gives leadership to you: in Christ you are unshakably on top. *Divine psychology is human psychology fulfilled.*

The Pastor Principle says every leader is a servant. The Church Principle makes servants into leaders too. European theologian Oscar Cullmann put it, in *Jesus and the Revolutionaries,* "Between the conversion of the individual and the reform of the structures, a reciprocal action is required."[39] Without the Church Principle of submission, the Pastor Principle of leadership produces a legalized Christian ethic, unenforceable and unenforced. Racial violence teaches us today that leadership alone is not enough. You either have submission or else you have society hamstrung, a prey for wolves.

"Time was invented by Almighty God to give ideas a chance," said Columbia University's president for forty-three years, Nicholas Murray Butler. Humanity is only beginning to comprehend the explosive power in Jesus of Nazareth's ideas. John Gardner says, "How many of us really recognize in modern life the seedlings of new ideas and new ways that will shape the future? The new thing rarely comes on with a flourish of trumpets. The historic innovation looks exciting in the history books, but if one could question those who lived at the time, the typical response would be neither 'I opposed it' nor 'I welcomed it,' but 'I didn't know it was happening.' "[40] Emil Brunner tells us the most politically potent thing any of us can do is to encourage genuine Christian discipleship.[41] Out from the Church spreads the Church Principle. Renewal within the Church is not "a" development within twentieth-century history; it *is* twentieth-century history. Holy history makes history.

Truth-Talk Bathed in Love

Consultant Marvin Bower listed four ways for expanding your group's, your organization's, or your family's *ability to innovate:*

(1) "Develop a fact-founded, objective approach to solving problems." (Truth-think gives you freedom from fearing the authorities, both those inside, and those outside your organization. St. John said, "Perfect love casts out fear."[42])

(2) "Separate long-range planning from short-term execution." (You do the task closest at hand—the providence of proximity—leaving long-range planning—eschatology—to God.)

(3) "Foster a desire to improve and a dissatisfaction with the status quo." (You keep your gaze fixed on Christ's perfection. He reminds you constantly of your own need to change the inward you.)

(4) "Create a working atmosphere within the organization that

leads to freedom of expression and to openness among people."[43] (Your truth-talk gets bathed in love, openness from the top-down, openness from the bottom-up.)

Dr. John Dillingham of Topeka's famous Menninger Foundation says, "Leadership is always a group phenomenon. . . . the same characteristics are needed by the members of the group as by their leader." Without the Church Principle, the Pastor Principle will not work. Love is a chain of command. In the original Greek the word for "submission" is *hupotasso*, from the military figure of speech "to line up under."[44] Leaders lined up under God make organizations lined up under leaders exciting. Marvin Bower says: "Innovation thrives in an atmosphere that stimulates people to express themselves freely and deal with each other in an open, non-political manner . . . through constructive leadership, not through 'clobberings' or crackdowns. The fear of rolling heads will not inspire innovation, it kills off ideas before their birth."[45] Turn truth-talk loose in relationships of love and you discover the power of Christ's sane thinking. You learn—as Peter Howard put it— that "ideas have legs."[46] The "gimme" idea of materialism is our crazy idea of revolt. Revolution is "gimme" from the bottom. Oppression is "gimme" from the top. The Prodigal Son, rebelling against his father, shouting "gimme," ran away from home. But he faced at last revolution's animality—in the far country's pigpen mud. He got up, he started home, he changed his mind, he "came to his senses." He said to his father: "Make me like one of your hired servants." The father welcomed him and threw a party—not for a servant, but for his son. Then the Elder Brother—who had not left home—started saying "gimme" too, his subterranean resentments for his father fanning his hate for his brother. In each of us is the Prodigal Son and the Elder Brother both. The Prodigal Son is "revolution *externalized,*" conscious. The Elder Brother is "revolution *internalized,*" subconscious. "Make me"—"make me what you want me to be" is always the answer. You get up and come to the suffering, waiting, wounded Father. The openness of Church-Principle-Communication makes for homecoming everyday.[47] You create around you a climate in which it is easy for people to change their minds. Organizational openness IS intellectual power.

Why We Appear Wasteful

Steiner says, "Creative organizations take more blind alleys, on the whole—recognizing them in time, of course—while less creative ones tend to take the safe, tried-and-true way. The creative organization often appears to be wasteful."[48] Looking at wastefulness you can get distracted. Some lessons are beyond economics. In his book *Self-Renewal*, John Gardner said, "It is essential that in the years ahead we undertake intensive analysis of the impact of the organization on the individual."[49] Such a study—to which I hope my book can contribute—will bring the Church her finest hour. Organization is Christ fighting on his battleground—the Team playing on its own home field. The only people who will endure as leaders are people free to be followers. In *The Organizational Revolution* Kenneth Boulding says, "In earlier days a neurotic personality merely had the power of making his wife and family miserable. He now has the power—if he is in a position of authority—to make a whole crew of subordinates (and even superiors) miserable. Unfortunately, neurotic personalities who are incapable of having satisfactory relationships with other people are apt to transfer their personal relationships into drive, aggressiveness, and ambition. They are, therefore, not unlikely to rise to positions of authority where the quieter and better adjusted persons remain unnoticed by their superiors."[50] As I repeat Dr. Boulding's words to you, I sit remembering the last verse of the first hymn we sang Sunday at Parkdale Church. William D. Longstaff (1822-1894) wrote it many years ago, and though I doubt Mr. Longstaff thought he was writing about our organizational crisis, he was:

> Take time to be holy,
> Be calm in thy soul;
> Each thought and each motive
> Beneath His control;
> Thus led by His Spirit
> To fountains of love,
> Thou soon shall be fitted
> For service above.

"Service above" most certainly means heaven. But it also means organizational heaven down here. "Service above" is indispensable to save the bureaucratic earth. Heavenly ideas—far from being wasteful—pay off in big ways.

By-Product Prosperity

Only blind men could miss the overpowering, inescapable fact that *what we call today the "have" nations of the world are those nations where there has been the most broadbased popular thinking about the Scriptures.* This fact is overwhelmingly obvious—denigrating the White Anglo-Saxon Protestant (WASP) we only trample it—as we try to adjust to our Western affluence. Even Oriental countries noted for their prosperity—like Japan—have followed, at least superficially, Western civilization's patterns. Does this mean that the "have" nations are better, somehow, than the "have-nots"? Of course not—it may mean just the opposite: "To whom much is given, of him shall much be required."[51] It calls us to honor Christ for, with, and by our material plenty. If we *achieved* it, our wealth becomes our idolatry. If we *received* it, it is an incentive for gratitude. Do we turn to God in order to get rich? Not unless we forsake the God and Father of our Lord Jesus Christ for the great god Mammon. Commit yourself to Christ and your primary riches are spiritual, intellectual, emotional, relational. You may or may not get rich financially. You may or may not stay that way. World economics prove to you in massive data, however, that collectively as well as individually Jesus fulfills his promise: "Seek first the Kingdom of God and his righteousness and I will add to you ALL THESE THINGS."[52] Prosperity comes only as a by-product. Put money first and it will rot in your hands.

Financial inequality—a continuing and inescapable problem— is what Jesus meant when he said, "The poor you have with you always."[53] Not that Christians have no concern about poverty, but that Christians are most realistic about what to do about it. If the problem of unequal incomes could be solved by revolution, *the world has never had a revolution yet.* Witness China or Russia today. Economist Kenneth Boulding points out the fallacy of Socialist economics: "It is simply not true that the main cause of poverty is exploitation. This is not to deny that exploitation exists. The main reason why people are poor, however, anywhere in the world, is not that they produce a lot and have it taken away from them. It is that they produce so pitiably little. . . . It is a tragedy that the wrong revolution is being peddled most actively—wrong in the sense that it is a revolution based on a wholly inadequate social science. It is not exploitation in the Marxist sense which is wrong with these [underdeveloped] countries; it is a lack of exploitation of opportunities for technical progress *because of the culture patterns of the dominant class.* "[54] Christian leadership is the realistic way to do something about world poverty. Will and Ariel Durant echo: "Violent revolutions do not so much redistribute wealth as destroy it. The only real revolution is the enlightenment of the mind and improvement of character, the only real emancipation is individual, and the only real revolutionists are philosophers and saints."[55]

Extravagance for Everyone

Revolutionary movements combine the idealistic and the demonic. Our task is to affirm their good ideals, resist their demonic strategy, and love the rebels themselves. Any blanket condemnation of modern hippie protest only reveals our Establishment rebellion. True rebellion is not necessarily in the protester, it may be in his self-righteous accuser. Red-necks are rebels just as much as hippies. Pay your money, take your choice, both are the same. Right-wingers and left-wingers together make revolution fly— rebellion fanned by repression. Satan's purpose strikes at faith— to destroy truth-think. The Bible calls Satan "the deceiver"— hitting at your truth-think to eliminate your truth-talk.[56] Alexander Solzhenitsyn, whom Simon Karlinsky in the *New York Times Book Review* says "is in a class by himself on the literary landscape of our age," speaks a word of Pastoral Authority to us in his Nobel prizewinner lecture: "Violence does not exist by itself and cannot do so; it is necessarily interwoven with lies. Violence finds its only refuge in falsehood, falsehood its only support in violence. Any man who has once acclaimed violence as his method must inexorably choose falsehood as his principle."[57] The Bible warns us: "Our sins testify against us, speaking Oppression and Revolt, uttering from the heart lying words, lacking truth."[58] "Oppression and Revolt" are the upper and lower prongs of Satan's pitchfork. Authority and Submission are the upper and lower beams of Christ's cross.

Some years ago I sat beside the swimming pool of a luxurious American hotel. I was to speak in a church nearby, a church whose membership was mostly rich. Beside me at poolside sat the church's pastor—cultured, personable, handsome. He had invited me—together with my laymen's team—to meet with his congregation. He had arranged for our hotel and hospitality. He proved a delightful host—but that particular day he was tense.

"Howard," he said, "I think it's wasteful of you to rent a parlor as well as a bedroom in this hotel. You don't need two rooms. You got them just to gratify your ego. You're not content with just a single room."

"I'm glad you've told me how you feel," I said. "You compliment our relationship with your honesty. But the truth is that my last trip (to another state) I only rented a single room. I didn't have a team with me there as I do here. We didn't need an extra room for team meetings." He paused, staring at me hard. My answer had unsettled him. Now it was my turn to question him. "Tell me," I said, "tell me how you feel about the house where you live —the house your congregation built for you. Do you feel guilty about it? Is it too plush?" I knew if he had guilt about his own living standards it would explain his condemnation of me.

"Maybe I do feel guilty," he said.

"Well, don't," I said. "If you pastored in a ghetto that house would be inappropriate, but not here. Give thanks for it. You've got to learn how to receive."

A mutual friend was sitting nearby. She spoke up. "Did it ever occur to you," she said to the pastor, "that God is extravagant?"

The pastor looked at her, bewildered.

"Look around." Her hand waved toward lush foliage, magnificent scenery, trees, flowers, and bright blue sky. "Look," she said. "It's lavish. God is no tightwad. He gave us unbelievable color and texture and splash." She sounded like Jeremiah on ecology: "Your wrongdoing has upset nature's order, your sins have kept you from her kindly gifts."[59] God lives it up . . . he's a big spender!

Do you remember the beautiful story in the Gospels about Mary's gift to Jesus of an alabaster box of perfume? It was love's extravagance. She broke this outrageously expensive fragrance—container and all—and poured it over his feet. Jesus did not rebuke Mary. He commended her. He said the story of her gift would be repeated endlessly. It has been. Mary was criticized, however, by Judas. She should have sold the perfume, said Judas, and given the money to the poor. Her act of extravagant, spontaneous, irrepressible love left Judas bewildered. His hostility hardened.[60]

For years my wife wanted a beautiful watch. I never got it for her. Jewelry I looked at askance. It was wasteful. (Fundamentalism's gnostic strains say that wealth, material things, even beauty itself, are evil.) Then I realized the psychological explanation. My family had never appreciated jewelry . . . but Barbara Dan's family loved it. Her father is a superb craftsman . . . his hobby is polishing rocks. My own family background was robbing my wife of an expression she needed of my love. So I changed my mind. I repented. I shopped. I spoke love to my wife in her language: the language of jewelry. She doesn't particularly like travel, but I'm always giving her trips. Now you should see her new watch. It sparkles in her eyes wherever we go—in either our single rooms or our fancy suites.

Submission (service) is power. If you ask a typical American businessman why he is in business, he will probably say, "To make a profit." He is right, of course, but he is right superficially. (Lots of us businessmen are not too good on our long-range thinking.) "The notion that profit is the objective of a business is beguiling," says Marvin Bower, "but it is often dangerous and self-defeating. The managers of any business will make better strategic decisions if they think of profit as a reward for *serving users well*—not so much as objective in itself as a yardstick of managerial effectiveness."[61] Harvard Business School dean Stanley Teele once described the American worker's high productivity. Overseas our productivity is admired, even envied. Dean Teele watched many teams come from abroad to study American industry, searching for our key. But most of these foreign visitors concentrated on the superficial, on the surface causes for our high productivity and missed the fundamentals. "Our industrial productivity stems from deep-seated matters of the spirit," he said, "rather than any surface, technical, or operating tricks." Dean Teele called his paper "Christian Productivity." What happens when you submit to your boss? Your submission makes him great. What happens in the process for you? Sharing his greatness you become greater yourself. You grow in his growth. Revolution does not create wealth but destroys it. American affluence and Third World poverty both call for submission.

Tonight I have been watching Billy Graham on television. He told of a spoiled little girl who attended his crusade. On her way into the meeting as she passed each policeman she stuck out her tongue. But at the close, as Billy gave the appeal, this very little girl came forward, committing her life to Christ. On the way home her attitude was different. As she passed each policeman she *smiled*. "A little child shall lead them."[62] Social health produces a healthy climate for economic progress, widespread. Class strife turns counter productive economically. In multifaced ways, Christian obedience contains practical and realistic help for people who are poor. The fastest way to change things—constructively—is to concentrate on Christian leadership. "The King's business requires such haste."[63] The strategy of Christ and his apostles was to concentrate on building—through Being—the Church.

Therapeutic Society: To Lead Is to Suffer

"The image created by the beatniks and by most of their predecessors back to the nineteenth century bohemians has led us to suppose that people of high originality are somehow lawless," says John Gardner. "The truly creative man is never an outlaw but a lawmaker. Every great creative performance since the first one has been in some measure a bringing of order out of chaos."[64]

Despair haunts American society. Oppressed by technocracy, besieged by revolution, is it rational for us to hope? Secular hope is vague, elusive, a vanishing will-o'-the-wisp. Today it is either undefined progress, violent revolution, or undifferentiated mysticism. Hope for the secularist quakes before the bomb, faints in each new crisis, dies with every war. Christian hope is clear, photographable, with definition and content. Today it turns again to the historic Jesus, the irresistible Bible, the eternal Church. Hope for the Christian rests in history past, makes history present, awaits history to come.

In 1512 Martin Luther was grasped by a transforming fact, "the just shall live by faith": it was a Word of Soul Liberty in an age of Church Oppression.

In 1738 John Wesley's inner being was strangely kindled at Aldersgate: it was a Word of Warmheartedness in an age of Cold Reason.

In 1973 a many-faceted groundswell of awakening rumbles around us: it is a Word of Organizational Love in an age of Chaotic Estrangement.

Emotional healing widespread awaits the recognition of Christ in you. If God is Suffering Love, your likeness to him appears in your willingness to suffer. Submission is the way you help your boss change, your husband, your parents, your government. The organizational crisis is God's voice calling us to radical Christian obedience now. The Church Principle means we change—truly change —only in our group. Your change changes everybody around you. You create a climate of change in others. I hear a skeptic's voice shout, "But, Howard, people don't change!" I say to you, sir, that you are speaking blasphemy. The only man who thinks that people don't change is the man who is not changing himself. Christian change is the world's greatest contagion. Every man who changes himself becomes an agent of change for others. Jesus makes us "fishers of men": it is inevitable.[65] Even the most insignificant Christian turns out to be a leader. Leadership is the name of the Christian game.

The Leader as Therapist

One of the new emphases in modern psychiatry is William Glasser's *Reality Therapy*. It is closely related to the transactional analysis of Eric Bere's *Games People Play* and Thomas Harris's *I'm O.K.—You're O.K.* Glasser redefines old psychiatric language. He does not talk about "illness," he talks about "irresponsibility." The therapist convinces his patient that his irresponsible behavior—what would ordinarily be called some technical "illness"—will not be accepted. He accepts the patient; he rejects his irresponsibility. Healthy behavior is responsible; irresponsible behavior is sick. The doctor asserts a more aggressively involved authority. He no longer listens to the patient on the couch passively. His therapy is "transactional." He confronts the patient with reality. He expects change. He insists on it.

Christian leadership is therapeutic authority too. The Christian leader refuses irresponsible behavior. He accepts the person; he rejects his irresponsibility. He loves the person in his organization enough to accept the pain of conflict with him. Irresponsibility ignored is not love; it is indifference. Accepting authority, willing to engage in loving conflict, becomes emotional healing.

The Church Principle is social therapeutics. Glasser says, "Our basic job as therapists is to become involved with the patient and then get him to face reality. When confronted with reality by the therapist with whom he is involved, the patient is forced again and again to decide whether or not he wishes to take the responsible path. Reality may be painful, it may be harsh, it may be dangerous, but it changes slowly. All any man can do is to struggle with it in a responsible way by doing right and enjoying the pleasure or suffering the pain that may follow."[66]

Two men with whom I've worked have been estranged. Our relationship has been organizational: I am the leader. How can I help these men toward reconciliation? I get them to talk; I pray; I hope; I speak the truth. Chiefly I suffer. They hurt the organization, they hurt me. To *lead* is to suffer. Why do my brother

Charles and I stand together today, reconciled? In the ultimate, by Christian love. In the immediate, by our suffering father. Dad gave me up in the day-to-day company routine rather than have his sons at odds. So Charles and I could both win, he took the pain. To lead is to *suffer*.

Suffering was the heart of Christ's therapy for us: the Shepherd Leadership Style. Suffering is the heart of our pastoral therapy with others. To lead is to suffer; to submit is to suffer: to be a Christian is to suffer. "We are God's heirs—who share Christ's inheritance with him—if we really suffer with him."[67] Healing all comes from Christ: "Who healeth all thy diseases."[68] From the cross flows cosmic health. The surgeon's skill, the researcher's test tubes, the diagnostician's insight, the vaccine's antibodies, the prescription's cure—all agents of Christ incognito. In the glistening glass and steel where Dr. Salk makes his discovery, in the primitive back-country where witch doctors dispense a herbicide, or in the mysterious cellular structure where your own body restores itself—the healing power is all the same. His name is Love.

A Community of Health

In *Motivation and Personality* the great Jewish scholar Abraham Maslow defines psychotherapy as "a good human relationship." He states my thesis: "a good friend or husband is one who feels free enough to offer the equivalent of analytic interpretations for our consideration. . . . A wholly proper part of the study of psychotherapy is examination of the everyday miracles produced by good marriages, good friendships, good parents, good jobs, good teachers, etc. Every good human being is an unconscious therapist. We should approve of this, encourage it, teach it. Every man who is kind, helpful, decent, psychologically democratic, affectionate, and warm, is a psychotherapeutic force."[69] Church authenticity turns sick societies healthy. "It is agreed by practically all therapists," says Maslow, "that when we trace a neurosis back to its beginnings we shall find with great frequency a deprivation of love in the early years. One thing that therapy does is to make it possible to receive and utilize the love that heals. Love is a basic need for healthy development of the human being. Just as an organism needs salt to attain health and avoid illness, so also does it need love for the same reason."[70] Love hurts. Therapeutic authority accepts its pain. Servant-kings fight; in a sick world they carry contagious health. Loving Authority is therapeutic conflict. Velvet-covered bricks come pill size for what ails you. "God makes us broken bread and poured out wine."[71]

Jesus Christ came to BE within us a new style of leadership. The Old Testament points to Jesus; to Christ in you yet above you:

> He was despised and shunned by men, a man of pain who knew what sickness was; like one from whom men turn with shuddering, He was despised, we took no heed of Him. And yet ours was the pain He bore, the sorrow He endured! We thought Him suffering from a stroke at God's own hand; yet He was wounded because we had sinned, 'twas our misdeeds that crushed Him; 'twas for our welfare that He was chastised, the blows that fell to Him have brought us healing. Like sheep we had all gone astray, we had each taken his own way, and on Him the Eternal laid the guilt of all of us. He was ill-treated, yet He bore it humbly, He never would complain, dumb as a sheep led to the slaughter, dumb as a ewe before the shearers. They did away with Him unjustly; and who heeded how He fell, torn from the land of the living, struck down for sins of ours? They laid Him in a felon's grave, and buried Him with criminals, though He was guilty of no violence nor had He uttered one false word. But the Eternal chose to vindicate His servant, rescuing His life from anguish; He let Him prosper to the full, in a posterity with life prolonged. Yes, many shall hold my servant blameless, since 'twas their guilt He bore. Therefore, shall He win victory, He shall succeed triumphantly, since He has shed His life-blood, and let Himself be numbered among rebels, bearing the great world's sins, and interposing for rebellious men.[72]

Isaiah saw him coming seven hundred years ahead. Two thousand years gone by, nearer now than when we first believed, you begin to see him freshly in his Church . . . the Leader's style in his universal group. Authority was, is, and will be forever Submission. "I, if I be lifted up from the earth will draw all men to myself."

Jesus said these words "to show by what death he was to die."[73] You get lifted up to your place of authority by means of the cross inside you. Henry James' heroine in *The Spoils of Poynton* was the "one person of intelligence in a collection of fools." Her secret was "a great accepted pain."[74] Alistair Cooke says James agreed with Jesus: "the great virtue is renunciation." Your pain accepted is your nobility. The lesson of the Maltese Cross: "I must be where my pain is. Only by accepting it can I overcome it." The community of health: submission accepted. This authority is the secret of society's healing. Dr. Maslow said, " 'The child must be loved' can read with equal validity 'The child must love.' "[75] Love flows both ways: down to the follower; up to the leader. The Church Principle makes you a therapeutic leader—by means of the creative way you follow.

Physicians all enter the practice of medicine by taking the Hippocratic Oath. Four centuries before Christ, this Greek physician we call "the father of medicine" described the experience of every man who sets out to BE a member of Christ's strong and healthy body in a sick and ailing world. Hippocrates said, "The life so short, the craft so long to learn."[76]

The Bible's name for velvet-covered bricks is *living stones*.[77] They do not come by human manufacture. The brick is all through the velvet and the velvet is all through the brick: velvet is submission, brick is authority; authority shot through with submission; submission shot through with authority. Nobody but God makes the two into one. Your submission without your authority is suicide; your authority without your submission is murder. The cross and the resurrection are submission and authority combined: Jesus Christ is our *Living Stone*.[78] Gentle granite, tender concrete: in human skin, Gibraltar. The Rock of Ages is Love. Christ in you is music: self-love and self-denial in rhythm. The Prophet, Priest, and King makes a prophet, a priest, and a king out of you.

Postscript

After the children were off to school this morning, Barbara Dan and I shared thoughts exploring our future—over two cups of hot tea turned cold. Our eldest son is leaving for college. Soon my wife must face the empty nest. She is a homebody, a nest-girl. Between us we dawdled the possibility that we might *not* travel in our later years, as once we had dreamed. My youthful visions had us striding in seven-league boots across the religious stage. Right now my modesty of outreach doesn't make me look like Gulliver; more often I feel like a middle-Lilliputian. What if our dream shrank to a tight little pucker of reality in one local, prosaic, right-here part of Texas? Any gospel that is not good news at breakfast over cold tea is not good news at all. If Corpus Christi turns out to be our boundary, then color this town *Excitement-for-Me*. God makes big worlds little and little worlds big; obedience is the secret; there are no little places anywhere.

> Let not our town be large, remembering
> That little Athens was the Muses' home,
> That Oxford rules the heart of London still,
> That Florence gave the Renaissance to Rome.[1]

The world was Wesley's parish—but it was the breadth of his vision, not the range of his horse that stretched it. Lord, help me learn the Unnoticed Life—quiet cups of cold water—whose only trumpet fanfare sounds from "the hid battlements of eternity." Jesus didn't get around too much; Nazareth was a little place.

O.K., Howard. One day at a time. Today I'm *right here*, writing. But I still feel like Colin Wilson's *Outsider*.

(1) *A businessman*, I feel "in" but not "of" the circle of ap-

proval, esteem, and camaraderie of men who "make it big." Why? Subjectively, is it the second-generation money? Or my distinction from Dad? Or Charles' role in our company? Objectively, does my style of life, my value system, form a barrier to my friends in the world of business? Using dollars to keep score, businessmen are players in a game called Money. As 'Adam Smith' says, "You could take all the trophies away and substitute plastic heads or whale's teeth; as long as there is a way to keep score, they will play."[2] Thanks to Dad, Charles, and H.E.B. I'm still scoring. But I'm not comfortable with the Bank as my Scorekeeper. Balance sheets leave too much unsaid. Red ink on a statement is a bad dream— being turned down for the loan a businessman's nightmare. 'Adam Smith' again: "If the occupation is money-making in its pure raw white form then anxiety must always be present. . . . 'Those who live by numbers can also perish by them. . . . The Witch of Wall Street is capricious, and by the rules of the game some men must end up on a barstool with a slip of adding machine tape in their slightly fraying $300 pockets, saying 00.00, Do Not Pass Go. . . .' 'When the identity card says, "He had Sperry at 16," or "He made 200 thou last year," or "He is worth a mil easy," then there are the seeds of a problem.' "[3] A problem, slightly . . . depression, despair, suicide, hell.

The financial world is no place to rest; I'm *in* but not *of* it. My critics call me a refugee. No. It's a question of where a Christian is directed to put his weight down. If God put me back in day-to-day business I could be happy there. But Christ being the Word, not the Numbers, I can't be bound to a balance sheet. Right now my schedule affirms: Business is not home.

(2) *A college trustee,* I am "in" but not "of" the world of education. The floodwaters of academic bankruptcy lap up to the edge and then wash over the floor of our society. Jacques Barzun urges radical school reform upon us; he suggests a Ph.D. at birth for every citizen. The generational storm threatens schoolhouse collapse. But still we hear idolatrous prattle that the great god Education will unravel all our social tangles. The imbecility of it nauseates me. Scholastic Superstition . . . Academic Pride ties up our souls. God, get us past Greece. Unslave our brains. Break the pink corpuscular chains. Christian integrity in Church Colleges

evaporates while we pant after the prosperity of the State Schools; like bitches in heat we lust for the Baal-Gods: Bigness, Prestige, Recognition. The mini-versity morass that results is explained to us solely in terms of finances: "Money would cure everything." Materialism is not unique to business. Clarity of purpose always answers our needs. Has "Christian education" in our day been clear? Springing out of our Faith comes a uniqueness and distinctiveness in our Identity. *Who* are we anyway? *Whose?*

Where will the new creative, contemporary Christian educational forms emerge for our day? *Prophetic Institutions* to serve this generation by the will of God? How will laymen be trained for Church History's new era? Dear God, give us an educational revival—take the dimness of our minds away. And help Outsiders like me persevere.

(3) *A churchman,* I am a man apart in the world of religion. I am too conservative for the liberals, too liberal for the conservatives, too unpredictable for the middle-of-the-roaders, too contemporary for the traditionalists, too old-fashioned for the avant-garde. My friendliness toward psychiatry and social involvement makes the old-line evangelicals suspicious; but my evangelism puts me out of step for the social-action crowd. The world-changers don't like my eschatology; the group-therapy addicts reject my Calvinism; the fundamentalists abhor my small-group openness. The Baptists fear my ecumenicity—the ecumenists avoid my independence—the independents suspect my churchmanship! Dear Lord, am I paranoid? Is everybody out to get me, even in your Church? Especially there? Of course not—it is the one place I am at home. But the world of religion and life in the Church are two different things. So I am in the religious world but not of it—reassured remembering: "Woe to you when all men speak well of you."[4] Penetrating the world, the Church is authentic. Otherwise it is not. Our true citizenship is in heaven; our Lord had most of his trouble with the world of religion. Quo vadis?

> This world is not my home,
> I'm just a passing through.
> My treasures are laid up
> Somewhere beyond the blue.[5]

It's a corny song. But BUTT, YOU BETTER BELIEVE IT:
down-to-earth Christianity requires heavenly minded Hope. Especially in church.

(4) *As a man in society,* I'm a fish out of water. High society
is not my world. Why not? In my dinner jacket I look like a
fourteen-carat socialite. Well, maybe it's my Baptist background.
Or the classic insecurity of the *nouveau riche.* Or do we teetotalers
make people uncomfortable by some chemical fragrance: the
buried memory of legal prohibition, for all party boys the Baptist's
B.O.? That B.O. feeling almost drives me to Bourbon Cologne.
Sometimes I'd like to smell like an alcoholic just to dispel the
long-lingering aroma of self-righteousness. Dad always took his
Coke in a bottle at our Food Industry cocktail parties lest anyone
think he was trifling with demon rum. I admired his courage. At
least I'm past that. I can hold my 7-Up-in-a-glass with the best of
'em. How do you convince others that you really are accepting,
approving, rejoicing in their freedom to drink? I figured writing
a book was one way. Total abstinence is not the 11th commandment: the decision is yours as an individual. Unfortunately all of
us don't see that yet. In deference to my weaker Baptist brothers,
whose conscience would be offended if I drank, I have no choice
but to pass. St. Paul's explanation to the Corinthians on why he
ate no meat is simple practicality. America still lives in a cultural
hangover from the 1920s. Here in the South local-option prohibition was strong up into the 40s and beyond. In some communities
where Baptists predominate the issue is still a hot one: Texas has
a sizable sprinkling of dry towns—islands of crusading abstinence
in the rise of a drinking man's sea. Sometimes my drinking friends,
gin-and-tonic in hand, are troubled by my virgin 7-Up. But I refuse
to let their problem become mine. I'm living in the present;
Baptists are still Baptists; I am bound by the conscience of my
less-than-mature brethren. Don't feel sorry for me—my bondage
is freely chosen. Baptist preachers are a little harder to love then
Episcopal priests, but not much. I still love cocktail parties. How
else can you see all your friends? I only pray my cronies not bound
to our pietistic community will enjoy their freedom to imbibe as
I enjoy my freedom to abstain. Freedom runs both ways.

Anyway, as much as we Swingers cherish the In life, I still feel Out. Isn't the whole genius of Society to assert its power to leave you Out even when you're In? Its leverage is Estrangement. Liquor is a Christian option—Shutting People Out isn't. Estrangement is a mod nickname for Hell. Knowing the *right* people, belonging to the *right* clubs, going to the *right* parties, Junior League social service, debutante glamour, the beauty of the ball: it is not enough. The Social Register lacks height. It's their world, not ours.

Face it, Howard. You don't fit anywhere.

It's true, I don't. Do I lament the fact? Of course not—*I rejoice in it.* It proves I was created for More, that my union with Christ is real, that I am only at home in God. "The son of man has nowhere to lay his head."[6]

Max Lerner observes that our society has "little patience with the 'marginal man' . . . the man-out-of-the-culture . . . the poet, the exotic, the dilettante, the political and social rebel, the Thoreau-like idler, the aesthete, the saint. . . ."[7] I don't know where I come on that list. Since every Christian is a *saint,* call me a "marginal man" right there. Because I identify like crazy with his next observation: "All that Americans ask of their people on the margin of the culture is for them to pursue their eccentricities privately. They provide them with a reluctant neglect, but only rarely do they relax the obvious and continuous disapproval of what clashes so deeply with the main currents of community energy."[8] In honor of Mr. Lerner I hereby name my opponent Mr. Reluctant Neglect. Disapproval I can stand—at least it acknowledges my existence. Neglect ignores me into oblivion.

Max Lerner's conclusion gave me a lift for a week:

"It is usually the innovator and the marginal man of the culture who achieves enough of a detachment from it to help. . . ."[9]

Jesus was the original Outsider—the inescapable Marginal Man —out to shift mankind to a new Center. A baby in a barn at Bethlehem became homeless that all men might come Home. Cheer up, Howard. Funks are for kicking. You ARE at home in business, education, religion, and society. In Christ you're always at home. Bruce Larson says there are only two kinds of people in the world: *Hosts and Guests.* Left to myself I revert to my original nature: the Obnoxious Guest—demanding attention, making a mess, creating trouble, craving service. But in Christ I am slowly becoming, like him, the Congenial Host—comfortable, at home, serving the guests, creating joy, paying attention to earth because heaven pays attention to me. In Christ we have arrived—the future has captured today—it is now In . . . to be Out.

When I've made more progress as a Christian I won't worry whether or not you like my book.

Forgive me, Lord Jesus.
Thank you that you do.
Amen.

Notes

The following abbreviations designating Scripture translations are used in the Notes:

Amplified   The Amplified Bible
Beck   The Beck New Testament in the Language of Today
Berkeley   The Berkeley Version in Modern English
G.N.F.M.M.   Good News for Modern Man
K.J.V.   The King James Version
L.B.   The Living Bible
Moffatt   The Moffatt Translation
N.A.S.   The New American Standard Bible
N.E.B.   The New English Bible
Phillips   The J. B. Phillips New Testament
R.S.V.   The Revised Standard Version
Williams   The Williams New Testament

Foreword

1. C. Northcote Parkinson, *Mrs. Parkinson's Law* (Boston: Houghton Mifflin Company, 1968), p. 123.
2. Rabindranath Tagore (1861–1941).

I Leadership Can't Work Undefined

1. Matthew 6:6 (K.J.V.).
2. Ephesians 5:21 (K.J.V.).
3. Matthew 28:18–19 (R.S.V.).
4. Eric Hoffer, *The Ordeal of Change* (New York: Harper & Row, 1963), p. 65.

II The Style of the Servant-King

1. Chester Barnard, *The Functions of the Executive* (Cambridge: Harvard University Press, 1938), pp. 170–171 (italics added).
2. *Ibid.*, p. 276 (italics added).
3. Boris Pasternak, *Dr. Zhivago* (New York: Pantheon Books, 1958), p. 43 (punctuation altered).
4. Matthew 2:1; Luke 2:1–2 (K.J.V., paraphrased).
5. Matthew 18:20 (K.J.V.).
6. John 6:35 (N.A.S.).
7. John 14:6 (K.J.V.).
8. John 8:58 (K.J.V.).
9. John 11:26 (K.J.V., paraphrased).
10. John 8:36 (N.A.S.).
11. Matthew 11:28 (K.J.V.).
12. Cf. C. S. Lewis, *Mere Christianity* (New York: The Macmillan Company, 1952), p. 41.
13. John 1:3 (K.J.V.).
14. John 1:1, 14 (R.S.V.).
15. Hebrews 13:8 (K.J.V.).
16. Miguel de Unamuno (1864–1936), Spanish philosopher.
17. Luke 22:29 (G.N.F.M.M.).
18. Ephesians 2:6 (G.N.F.M.M.).
19. Revelation 5:10 (G.N.F.M.M.).
20. I Corinthians 15:25 (K.J.V.).
21. George Eldon Ladd, *The Gospel of the Kingdom* (Grand Rapids: Wm. B. Eerdmans, 1959), p. 117.
22. I John 4:17 (K.J.V.).
23. Revelation 3:11 (N.E.B.).
24. Matthew 6:9 (K.J.V.).
25. Philippians 2:6f. (N.E.B.).
26. C. S. Lewis, *op. cit.*, p. 136.
27. Proverbs 13:12 (R.S.V.).
28. Jürgen Moltmann, *Theology of Hope* (New York: Harper & Row, 1967), p. 23.

29. Acts 1:11 (PHILLIPS).

30. John 19:19 (K.J.V.).

31. James S. Stewart, *The Gates of New Life* (Edinburgh: T. & T. Clark, 1937), pp. 43, 46, 49.

32. Will Durant, *The Story of Civilization: Our Oriental Heritage* (New York: Simon & Schuster, 1942), p. 22.

33. Micah 5:2 (R.S.V.).

34. Zechariah 11:12 (K.J.V.).

35. Isaiah 50:5–6; 53:3, 5; 52:7, 13, 15 (R.S.V.).

36. John 16:13–14 (K.J.V.).

37. Romans 8:9 (G.N.F.M.M.).

38. Quoted by F.B. Warrick, M.D., Richmond, Indiana.

39. Lawrence J. Peter and Raymond Hull, *The Peter Principle* (New York: William Morrow, 1969), pp. 25, 9.

40. Mark 9:35; Luke 22:27 (N.A.S., paraphrased).

41. Ephesians 4:26 (K.J.V.).

42. Ephesians 4:15 (K.J.V.).

III Love: Authority That Wins

1. Robert T. Golembiewski, *Men, Management, and Morality* (New York: McGraw-Hill, 1965), p. 291.

2. Colossians 2:9 (K.J.V.).

3. Fred Hechinger, *Change* magazine, Winter 1971–1972.

4. Ephesians 6:9, paraphrased.

5. Peter Drucker, *The Effective Executive* (New York: Harper & Row, 1967), p. 53.

6. "The Blue-Collar Worker's Lowdown Blues," *Time* magazine, November 9, 1970, pp. 73–74.

7. James 1:27 (G.N.F.M.M. and Beck).

8. Abraham Maslow, *Motivation and Personality* (New York: Harper & Row, 1970), pp. 297–298.

9. Matthew 6:22 (K.J.V.).

10. Matthew 5:3–11 (K.J.V. and Phillips).

11. Matthew 7:29 (K.J.V., order reversed).

12. Matthew 10:39 (K.J.V.).

13. I John 4:18 (R.S.V.).

14. Genesis 1:28 (Berkeley).
15. William Glasser, *Reality Therapy* (New York: Harper & Row, 1965), p. 16.
16. *Ibid.*, p. 88.
17. *Ibid.*, pp. 18–19.
18. John 19:11 (G.N.F.M.M.).
19. Romans 5:1 (K.J.V.).
20. Revelation 13:8; I Corinthians 13:4 (K.J.V.).
21. Hebrews 2:10 (N.E.B.).
22. II Corinthians 5:19 (R.S.V.).
23. Hosea 11:8, 9 (R.S.V.).
24. II Corinthians 1:3 (K.J.V.).
25. Acts 1:8 (K.J.V.).
26. C. S. Lewis, *George Macdonald* (New York: The Macmillan Company, 1947), p. 118.
27. II Corinthians 1:5–7 (R.S.V.).
28. Oswald Chambers, *My Utmost for His Highest* (New York: Dodd, Mead, 1935), p. 7.
29. Matthew 25:34–40
30. John 14:16, 26; 15:26; 16:7 (K.J.V.).
31. I John 2:1 (N.E.B.); Also see A. T. Robertson, *Word Pictures in the New Testament* (New York: Harper & Brothers, 1932), Vol. V, p. 252.
32. Romans 6:11, paraphrased.
33. I Corinthians 13:7 (R.S.V.).
34. John 8:11; Mark 5:34; John 5:8 (K.J.V.).
35. Romans 8:1 (R.S.V.).
36. From Dr. Paul Musselman, director of the Division of Evangelism, National Council of Churches, in personal conversations as well as from this story.
37. Golembiewski, *op. cit.*, pp. 275–276.
38. Carl Rogers, *Freedom to Learn* (Columbus, Ohio: Charles E. Merrill Publishing Company, 1969), pp. 74ff.
39. Rensis Likert, *New Patterns of Management* (New York: McGraw-Hill, 1961), pp. 179, 58.
40. John 15:14–15; John 15:13 (R.S.V.).

41. II Corinthians 5:21; Philippians 2:7 (K.J.V.).
42. Mark 15:37 (G.N.F.M.M.).
43. *The Westminster Larger Catechism*, 1861 (Richmond, Virginia: John Knox Press).
44. II Corinthians 4:5 (K.J.V.).
45. Proverbs 28:13 (R.S.V.).
46. Psalm 76:10.
47. John Bowring (1792–1872), *Baptist Hymnal* (Nashville: Convention Press, 1956), p. 100.
48. I John 4:8 (K.J.V.).
49. James 5:16 (R.S.V.).
50. James 5:20 (R.S.V.).
51. Karl Olsson, former president, North Park College and Seminary; now leadership development director, Faith at Work.
52. Titus 3:5 (K.J.V.).
53. II Corinthians 12:10. (K.J.V)
54. Matthew 5:3 (K.J.V., paraphrased).
55. Bruce Larson, *Dare to Live Now* (Grand Rapids: Zondervan, 1965), chap. 3.
56. Likert, *op. cit.*, p. 175.
57. Marvin Bower, *The Will to Manage* (New York: McGraw-Hill, 1966), page 149.
58. Romans 3:23 (K.J.V.).
59. John 16:33 (K.J.V., italics added).
60. Matthew 6:12, paraphrased.
61. I Corinthians 1:30 (K.J.V.).
62. Matthew 18:22 (K.J.V., paraphrased).
63. Matthew 18:15 (N.E.B.).
64. Matthew 5:23–24 (N.E.B.).
65. Ephesians 4:26 (K.J.V.).
66. Ephesians 4:26 (K.J.V.).
67. Philippians 2:4 (N.E.B.).
68. Robert Frost, "A Cabin in the Clearing," *In the Clearing* (New York: Holt, Rinehart and Winston, 1962), p. 17.

IV Submission: Key to Power

1. Philippians 2:9 (k.j.v.).
2. I Samuel 15:24 (r.s.v.).
3. I Samuel 15:17 (r.s.v.).
4. I Samuel 15:12 (r.s.v.).
5. I Samuel 15:26 (r.s.v.).
6. I Samuel 15:22 (l.b.).
7. I Samuel 31:4 (r.s.v.).
8. I Samuel 15:22–23 (l.b.).
9. I Samuel 26:5–11 (l.b.).
10. I Samuel 26:22–23 (l.b.).
11. Romans 13:1–2 (r.s.v.).
12. Romans 13:4, 6 (r.s.v.).
13. Titus 2:15–3:2 (r.s.v.).
14. I Peter 2:13, 18; 3:1; 5:5 (r.s.v.).
15. I Peter 5:6 (r.s.v.).
16. From a letter to Malesherbes, January 12, 1792, reproduced in John Morley, *Rousseau and His Era* (London: Harper & Brothers, 1923), Vol. I, p. 127; quoted by Will and Ariel Durant, *Rousseau and Revolution* (New York: Simon & Schuster, 1967), p. 19 (Italics added).
17. Romans 3:10 (l.b.).
18. Luke 18:19 (n.e.b.).
19. Will and Ariel Durant, *Rousseau and Revolution*, p. 899.
20. Edmund Burke, "Letter to a Member of the National Assembly," in *Reflections on the French Revolution*, quoted by Will and Ariel Durant, *op. cit.*, p. 891.
21. John 1:1 (k.j.v.).
22. Will and Ariel Durant, *op. cit.*, p. 890.
23. *Ibid.*, pp. 178, 17, 9.
24. *Ibid.*, p. 890.
25. E. P. Hollander, *Leaders, Groups and Influence* (New York: Oxford University Press, 1964), p. 1.
26. *Ibid.*, pp. 23, 25–26.

27. John 15:14–15 (R.S.V.).
28. Hebrews 9:27 (K.J.V.).
29. Galatians 2:20 (K.J.V.).
30. Hollander, *op. cit.*, p. 19.
31. This thought comes from Barnard, *op. cit.*, p. 163.
32. *Ibid.*, p. 184.
33. Paul Torgersen, *A Concept of Organization* (New York: American Book-Van Nostrand, 1969), p. 113.
34. Barnard, *The Functions of the Executive, pp. 136, 259.*
35. Emil Brunner, *Christianity and Civilisation* (New York: Scribners, 1948), p. 138.
36. Plato, *The Republic,* Book VIII, line 545.
37. Sylvia and Benjamin Selekman, *Power and Morality in a Business Society* (New York: McGraw-Hill, 1956), p. vii, quoted by Golembiewski, *Men, Management, and Morality, page 57.*
38. Cf. Hollander, *op. cit.*, pp. 33–34.
39. Johann Wolfgang von Goethe (1749–1832), quoted in W. H. Auden and Louis Kronenberger, eds. *The Viking Book of Aphorisms* (New York: Viking Press 1962), p. 137
40. Torgersen, *op. cit.*, page 54 (italics mine).
41. Clyde Reid, *Celebrate the Temporary* (New York: Harper & Row, 1972).
42. Luke 9:51, paraphrased.
43. Ephesians 5:21; James 4:7 (K.J.V.).
44. Galatians 3:8 (K.J.V.).
45. Hollander, *op. cit.*, page 11.
46. Hannah Arendt, *On Violence* (New York: Harcourt, Brace & World, 1969), p. 11.
47. I Peter 5:6 (K.J.V.).
48. Matthew 5:5 (K.J.V.).
49. Mark 15:6 (L.B.).
50. Mark 15:15 (N.E.B.).
51. Matthew 27:17; John 18:40; Mark 15:7 (R.S.V.).
52. Matthew 27:15 (R.S.V., footnote).
53. Mark 10:36–37 (R.S.V.).

54. Mark 10:51 (R.S.V.).
55. Proverbs 27:6; 28:23 (R.S.V.).

V The White Flag of Victory

1. Michael Glenny, "Alexander Solzhenitsyn and the Epic Tradition," *Harper's* magazine, Vol. 245, No. 1467, August 1972, p. 52.
2. Hannah Arendt, *The Origins of Totalitarianism* (New York: Harcourt, Brace and World, 1966), pp. 371, 387.
3. *Ibid.*, pp. 323, 322, 323.
4. Norman Grubb.
5. Philippians 2:3 (Phillips).
6. Philippians 2:5 (N.E.B.).
7. Philippians 2:12 (G.N.F.M.M.).
8. Philippians 3:17; 4:9 (N.E.B.).
9. II Corinthians 1:3ff.
10. Ephesians 6:12 (K.J.V.).
11. John Milton, *Paradise Lost*, Book 1, line 263.
12. Genesis 3:5 (K.J.V.).
13. John 8:44 (R.S.V.).
14. Matthew 7:1 (K.J.V.).
15. Romans 7:18; Isaiah 64:6; Luke 18:13 (K.J.V.).
16. John 19:11 (G.N.F.M.M.).
17. Matthew 19:24–26 (K.J.V.).
18. Matthew 5:3 (K.J.V.).
19. I Corinthians 13:11 (K.J.V.).
20. I Corinthians 13:5 (R.S.V.).
21. I Corinthians 13:4 (K.J.V.).
22. John 8:58 (K.J.V.).
23. *The Acts of Paul and Thecla*, the Armen. vers. #3, from Conybeare's Monuments, page 62, quoted in *Hastings Dictionary of the Bible*, (New York: Scribners, 1948)p. 691. Cf. II Corinthians 12:10.
24. Acts 16:11–40. (K.J.V.).
25. Galatians 3:24 (K.J.V.).
26. Romans 8:3–4 (G.N.F.M.M.).

27. Romans 8:3 (K.J.V.).
28. Romans 6:23; Ephesians 2:8–9 (K.J.V.).
29. Galatians 2:20 (K.J.V.).
30. I Corinthians 4:16; 11:1 (R.S.V.).
31. I Corinthians 11:1, paraphrased.
32. Matthew 6:25–33 (K.J.V.).
33. John 8:34 (K.J.V.).
34. John 5:41, 44 (Phillips).
35. John 8:28; 14:10 (N.E.B., italics added).
36. Revelation 3:20 (K.J.V.).
37. John 7:17 (Phillips).
38. Romans 12:2 (K.J.V.).
39. Maltz, *Psycho-Cybernetics* (Englewood Cliffs, New Jersey: Prentice Hall, 1960), pp. 44–45, 49.
40. Acts 9:5 (R.S.V.).
41. II Corinthians 10:5 (K.J.V.); Robert Browning (1812–1889), *A Woman's Last Word*, stanza 7.
42. I Corinthians 2:16 (K.J.V.).
43. Romans 8:5–6 (G.N.F.M.M.).
44. Romans 8:28–30 (K.J.V.).
45. John P. Sisk, "Honesty as a Policy," *The American Scholar*, Spring 1972, Vol. 41, No. 2, pp. 259–260.
46. Genesis 2:24 (K.J.V., italics added).
47. I Corinthians 11:28, 31 (Beck).
48. John 7:26, 48 (Phillips).
49. Galatians 6:14 (K.J.V.).
50. John 6:28–29 (N.E.B., italics added).

VI The God of the Ordinary

1. This thought came from Keith Miller.
2. Cf. Matthew 13:5–6.
3. Richard Halverson, *Between Sundays* (Grand Rapids: Zondervan, 1965).
4. Psalm 46:10 (R.S.V.).
5. Matthew 6:6 (R.S.V.).
6. Exodus 3:1–7, paraphrased.

180 THE VELVET COVERED BRICK

7. Gwyneth Cravens, "Hitching Nowhere: The Aging Young on the Endless Road," *Harper's* magazine, Vol. 245, No. 1468, September 1972, p. 67.
8. John 8:32 (Williams).
9. I Corinthians 11:27–28 (Beck).
10. Matthew 6:21 (G.N.F.M.M.).
11. Cf. Matthew 5:17 (K.J.V.).
12. Ephesians 3:17 (Dr. Robert Boyd Munger paraphrase).
13. Mark 9:43 (R.S.V.).
14. Oswald Chambers, *My Utmost for His Highest,* p. 114.
15. II Corinthians 6:2 (K.J.V.).
16. Colossians 2:6 (L.B.).
17. Colossians 2:10 (N.E.B.).
18. Keith Miller, *The Taste of New Wine* (Waco: Word Books, 1965), p. 99.
19. Samuel Shoemaker, *How to Become a Christian* (New York: Harper & Row, 1953), p. 71.
20. Colossians 2:6 (N.A.S.).
21. Chambers, *op. cit.*, p. 342.
22. Isaiah 35:1 (K.J.V., paraphrased).
23. Elizabeth Barrett Browning, *Aurora Leigh,* Book VII, line 820.
24. Ecclesiastes 9:10 (R.S.V.).
25. Mark 1:15 (R.S.V.).
26. Acts 20:21 (R.S.V.).
27. Hebrews 11:1 (K.J.V.).
28. Hebrews 11:1 (G.N.F.M.M.).
29. I Corinthians 3:21; II Corinthians 5:17–18 (K.J.V.).
30. I Corinthians 10:30 (G.N.F.M.M.).
31. Genesis 28:17 (K.J.V.).
32. Matthew 6:34, paraphrased.
33. Luke 18:1; I Thessalonians 5:17 (G.N.F.M.M.; K.J.V.; Beck).
34. From Dr. James Packer's lectures, Laity Lodge, August 1972.
35. John 1:1, 14 (K.J.V.).
36. Cf. Chambers, *op. cit.*, p. 48.
37. Romans 7:18, paraphrased.

38. "Raw faith" is a phrase introduced to me by Gene Warr, Christian layman of Oklahoma City.
39. Isaiah 40:31 (k.j.v.).
40. Dr. Ray Stedman and Dr. James Packer both contributed to these thoughts.
41. See A. T. Robertson, *Word Pictures in the New Testament*, Vol. IV, (New York: Harper & Brothers, 1931), p. 489; and J. H. Thayer, *Greek-English Lexicon of the New Testament* (New York: Harper & Brothers, 1889), pp. 484, 504.
42. Ian Thomas, *The Saving Life of Christ* (Grand Rapids: Zondervan, 1961), p. 61.
43. I Corinthians 13:13 (r.s.v.).

VII The Pastor Principle for Every Leader

1. Psalm 19:10 (l.b.).
2. I Corinthians 15:3–4 (r.s.v.).
3. Colossians 3:3 (k.j.v.).
4. Ephesians 4:15 (k.j.v.).
5. Dr. Ray Stedman, Laity Lodge, Summer 1972.
6. Galatians 6:5, 2 (k.j.v.).
7. I John 1:7, 9 (r.s.v.).
8. Hebrews 12:2 (r.s.v., italics added).
9. Philippians 2:13 (l.b.).
10. Philippians 2:12–13 (k.j.v.).
11. Psalm 40:8 (k.j.v.).
12. Mark 1:12–13 (r.s.v.).
13. Luke 8:29 (r.s.v.).
14. Luke 4:1–2 (r.s.v.).
15. Jeremiah 31:3 (l.b.).
16. Hebrews 2:10 (n.e.b.).
17. Oswald Chambers, *My Utmost for His Highest, op. cit.,* p. 124.
18. Psalm 75:7 (n.e.b.).
19. Marvin Bower, *The Will to Manage* (New York: McGraw-Hill, 1966), pp. 12–13.

20. Rensis Likert, *New Patterns of Management* (New York: McGraw-Hill, 1961), pp. 170, 14.
21. David M. Ogilvy, "The Creative Chef," in Gary A. Steiner, ed., *The Creative Organization* (Chicago: University of Chicago Press, 1965), p. 207.
22. *Phillips Brooks Lectures on Preaching*, quoted in *The Interpreter's Bible* (Nashville, Abingdon Press, 1952), Vol. VIII, p. 708.
23. William Barclay, *New Testament Words* (London: SCM Press, 1964), pp. 220–221.
24. John 1:1 (K.J.V.).
25. Revelation 19:15 (K.J.V.).
26. I John 4:17 (K.J.V.).
27. I John 5:5 (G.N.F.M.M.).
28. Revelation 22:3, 5 (R.S.V.).
29. I Corinthians 4:1 (Beck).
30. Mark 4:26–28 (G.N.F.M.M., italics added).
31. Ephesians 3:12, paraphrased.
32. Philippians 2:6, paraphrased.
33. Genesis 1:27 (K.J.V.).
34. II Corinthians 5:17 (R.S.V., italics added).
35. John 17:6 (K.J.V.).
36. Colossians 1:24 (R.S.V.).
37. Proverbs 10:24 (R.S.V.).
38. Matthew 19:19 (R.S.V.).
39. Philippians 2:7 (K.J.V.; Williams; N.E.B.; Phillips; R.S.V.).
40. Drucker, *The Effective Executive* op.cit., pp. 37–38.
41. John 14:12 (R.S.V.).
42. Galatians 5:13 (Phillips).
43. Oswald Chambers, *op. cit.*, p. 29.
44. Matthew 27:46; Mark 15:34 (K.J.V.).
45. Chambers, *op. cit.*, p. 30.
46. *Ibid.*, p. 78.
47. Luke 23:46 (R.S.V., italics added).
48. George Jean Nathan, *The Theatre in the Fifties*, quoted in Cliffton Fadiman, ed., *The American Treasury* (New York: Harper & Row, 1955), p. 902.

49. William Barclay, *New Testament Words* (London: SCM Press, 1964), p. 220.
50. Romans 12:12 (G.N.F.M.M.).
51. Cf. Hebrews 13:20; Romans 15:33; 16:20; II Corinthians 13:11; Philippians 4:9; I Thessalonians 5:23 (K.J.V.).
52. Colossians 3:15 (K.J.V.).
53. Philippians 4:6–7 (N.E.B.).
54. Luke 21:19 (K.J.V.).
55. Thought taken from Lewis, *George Macdonald*, "Light," *op. cit.*, pp. 88–89.
56. John 14:27 (R.S.V.).
57. John 14:16; II Thessalonians 3:16; Romans 14:17 (R.S.V.).
58. Hollander, *Leaders, Groups and Influence*, pp. 12–13.
59. Francis Thompson, "The Hound of Heaven," *The Oxford Book of Christian Verse* (Oxford: Clarendon Press, 1940), p. 510.

VIII The Church Principle for Every Organization

1. John 12:3–8; Galatians 2:10 (K.J.V.).
2. Gary A. Steiner, ed., *The Creative Organization* (Chicago: University of Chicago Press, 1965), p. 259.
3. Ephesians 2:14 (K.J.V.).
4. Matthew 23:9 (R.S.V.).
5. Revelation 21:8 (G.N.F.M.M.).
6. John 16:33 (K.J.V.).
7. Matthew 10:34 (R.S.V.).
8. II Corinthians 1:20 (K.J.V.).
9. Steiner, *op. cit.*, p. 259.
10. John 15:18; James 4:4 (R.S.V.).
11. Ephesians 4:26 (K.J.V.).
12. John 10:30 (R.S.V.).
13. John 5:6; Matthew 5:48 (K.J.V.).
14. Chambers, *My Utmost for His Highest*, p. 164.
15. Philippians 2:12–13 (K.J.V.).
16. Kahlil Gibran, "On Work," *The Prophet* (New York: Alfred A. Knopf, 1923, 1958), p. 28.

17. Matthew 17:5 (k.j.v.).
18. Sayers, *op. cit.*, p. 57.
19. Colossians 3:23 (g.n.f.m.m.).
20. Genesis 2:3 (r.s.v.).
21. Wayne Oates, *Confessions of a Workaholic* (New York: World Publishing Company, 1971).
22. Matthew 11:28ff. (n.a.s.).
23. John 19:23 (k.j.v.).
24. Isaiah 28:16 (r.s.v.).
25. David Ogilvy, "The Creative Person in Organizations," in Steiner, ed., *The Creative Organization*, p. 48.
26. Jerome Bruner, "The Creative Chef," in Steiner, ed., *op. cit.*, p. 210.
27. Steiner, "Concluding Remarks," in Steiner, ed., *op. cit.*, p. 259.
28. Hebrews 12:2 (r.s.v.).
29. Herbert Butterfield, *Christianity and History* (New York: Scribners, 1949), p. 104.
30. William Blake, *Jerusalem* (1804–1820), Ch. 1, preface.
31. Thomas Carlyle (1795–1881). Literally, "Genius . . . which is the transcendent capacity for taking trouble first of all," in *Life of Frederick the Great*, Book IV, chap. 3.
32. Dag Hammarskjöld, *Markings*, trans. Sjöberg and Auden (New York: Alfred A. Knopf, 1964), p. 133.
33. Paul Tournier, *To Resist or to Surrender* (Richmond, Virginia: John Knox Press, 1967), p. 13.
34. *Ibid.*, pp. 5–7.
35. Steiner, "Concluding Remarks," in Steiner, ed., *op. cit.*, p. 259.
36. Philippians 3:12 (Phillips).
37. T. S. Eliot, *The Cocktail Party* (New York: Harcourt, Brace & World, 1950), p. 118.
38. Matthew 10:39 (r.s.v.).
39. Oscar Cullmann, *Jesus and the Revolutionaries* (New York: Harper & Row, 1970), p. 55.
40. John W. Gardner, *Self-Renewal* (New York: Harper & Row, 1963), p. 29.

41. Cf. Emil Brunner, "Christian Responsibility in a World of Power," *The Church and the International Disorder* (New York: Harper & Brothers, 1948), p. 199.
42. I John 4:18 (R.S.V.).
43. Marvin Bower, "Nurturing Innovation," in Steiner, ed., *op. cit.*, p. 173.
44. Robertson, *Word Pictures in the New Testament, op. cit.*, Vol. IV, p. 544.
45. Bower, *op. cit.*, in Steiner, ed., *op. cit.*, pp. 177, 176.
46. Peter Howard, *Ideas Have Legs* (New York: Coward-McCann, 1946).
47. Luke 15:11–32 (G.N.F.M.M.).
48. Steiner, *op. cit.*, p. 259.
49. Gardner, *op. cit.*, p. 64.
50. Kenneth E. Boulding, *The Organizational Revolution* (Chicago: Quadrangle Books, 1968), p. 53.
51. Luke 12:48 (R.S.V.).
52. Matthew 6:33, paraphrased.
53. Mark 14:7 (K.J.V.).
54. Boulding, *op. cit.*, pp. 171–172 (italics added).
55. Will and Ariel Durant, *The Lessons of History* (New York: Simon & Schuster, 1968), p. 72.
56. Revelation 12:9 (R.S.V.).
57. *Time* magazine, September 4, 1972, p. 33.
58. Isaiah 59:12–15 (R.S.V., excerpted).
59. Cf. Jeremiah 5:25 (R.S.V.).
60. John 12:3–8; Matthew 26:7–13; Mark 14:3–9.
61. Bower, *op. cit.*, *The Will to Manage* (New York: McGraw-Hill, 1966), p. 61 (italics added).
62. Isaiah 11:6 (K.J.V.)
63. I Samuel 21:8 (adapted from L.B.).
64. Gardner, *op. cit.*, p. 39.
65. Mark 1:17 (R.S.V.).
66. Glasser, *Reality Therapy*, p. 41.
67. Romans 8:17 (Beck).
68. Psalm 103:3 (K.J.V.).
69. Maslow, *Motivation and Personality*, pp. 248, 249, 254.

70. *Ibid.*, pp. 275–276.
71. Chambers, *op. cit.*, p. 33.
72. Isaiah 53:3–12 (Moffatt).
73. John 12:32–33 (R.S.V.).
74. Henry James, *The Spoils of Poynton* (Norfolk, Connecticut: The New Classics Series, 1896–1924), p. 303. Also as quoted by Alistair Cooke, Masterpiece Theater, NET Television, Summer 1972.
75. Maslow, *op. cit.*, p. 250.
76. Hippocrates (460–357 B.C.), *Aphorisms, Sec I, Line 1.*
77. I Peter 2:5 (N.E.B.).
78. I Peter 2:4 (N.E.B.).

Postscript

1. Vachel Lindsay, *Selected Poems*, "On the Building of Springfield" (New York: The Macmillian Company, 1925), p. 74.
2. "Adam Smith," *The Money Game* (New York: Random House, 1967), p. 14.
3. *Ibid.*, pp. 78, 84, 95.
4. Luke 6:26 (R.S.V.).
5. Charles E. Fuller, H. Leland Green, William MacDougall, compilers, *Old Fashioned Revival Hour Songs* (Winona Lake, Indiana: Rodeheaver, Hall Mack, 1950), p.4.
6.. Matthew 8:20 (R.S.V.).
7. Max Lerner, *America as a Civilization* (New York: Simon and Schuster, 1957), pp. 545–546.
8. *Ibid.*, p. 546.
9. *Ibid.*, p. 549.

Acknowledgments

To my many pastors, both congregational and personal, whose lives begot in me this understanding of being a pastor myself.

To Tadashi Akaishi, Donald Cutler, Clayton Carlson, and Davis Yeuell, my pastor-editors.

To Wayne Oates and David Hubbard for invaluable suggestions.

To Leonard Holloway, my Executive Assistant, who came to Christian Men, Inc. from heaven via Sam Fore, Harold Kellum, and two college presidencies, enabling me to write this book.

To Dorothy Parish, my secretary, whose burning bush is a typewriter.

To Barbara Dan, my wife, with whom manuscripts and marriage are both fun.

DATE DUE

JOSTEN'S 30 508

6478